Praise for
What's the Big Deal about Pornography?

"Jill Manning's book is brutally honest about the proliferation of pornography in today's culture and the tragic effects it has on the lives of men, women, and children. But she offers hope and real help, too. *What's the Big Deal about Pornography: A Guide for the Internet Generation* provides concrete steps that can be taken to reclaim your life and free your family from pornography's destructive power."

—*Rebecca Hagelin, author of* Home Invasion: Protecting Your Family in a Culture That's Gone Stark Raving Mad

"This book should be in every home! It contains vital information essential for our fight against pornography. It begins with the basics and helps arm us with a concrete battle plan for parents as well as teens."

—*Cindy Moreno, president, Communities for Decency*

"The crass commercialization of sex in our culture has permeated the lives of our youth. This book is one of the first and necessary resources to effectively address the issue of pornography with young adults. Jill Manning brings her expertise, understanding, and a message of recovery and hope to a national audience in her usual compassionate and approachable style."

—*Donna Rice Hughes, chairman and president of Enough Is Enough; Internet safety author and speaker*

"In a world filled , this book offers clear direc good decisions about por d it. Additionally, Dr. Ma h to

recovery for those who already find pornography use addictive. *What's the Big Deal about Pornography* is a great resource for young people, parents, and youth counselors. I highly recommend this book."

—*M. Deborah Corley, Ph.D., LMFT, cofounder and clinical consultant for Santé Center for Healing*

"This book is brilliant! It is very timely, much needed, and offers an easy-to-read and common-sense approach to a very challenging, sensitive topic. I highly recommend it for young adults, parents, educators, and concerned citizens alike. Reading the book allows one to have a superb experience of discovering ways to help!"

—*Pamela J. Atkinson, president, Utah Coalition Against Pornography*

"In her straightforward, down-to-earth style, Jill Manning provides astonishing information about the dangers of pornography while at the same time empowering the reader with knowledge, hope, and realistic strategies for action. This is a must-read for every adolescent, young adult, and parent."

—*Todd Olson, LCSW, program director of LifeSTAR Network*

"This book is a timely resource that addresses the issue of pornography with clarity and honesty, as well as with caring and compassion. Parents, educators, counselors, and all those who care about the welfare of young people today will find this book to be a very effective tool."

—*Susan E. McAsey, high school teacher, Calgary, Alberta, Canada*

"Dr. Manning's work represents a monumental Rosetta Stone to help young men and women decipher sexual truth in a world saturated with pornographic messages that promote fraudulent messages about human intimacy. Her writing appeals to a broad audience from youth to parents, offering readers a refreshing perspective that will empower them to make healthy sexual decisions in their lives."

—*Rory C. Reid, licensed psychotherapist, coauthor of* Confronting Your Spouse's Pornography Problem

"Extremely well-written, informative, and easy-to-read. This isn't a book that should simply be 'found on every family's shelf'—but rather one that should be opened, with all family members present, learning from its informative pages. Manning candidly and sensitively addresses what all youth and families need to know about the dangers of pornography—in all of their subtlety. This thought-provoking book is a must-read for all families striving to live lives of purity in an open-access world."

—*Kyle S. Gillett, Ph.D., LMFT, assistant clinical director and research director, Telos Residential Treatment Center*

What's the
Big Deal
about
Pornography?

What's the
Big Deal
about
Pornography?

A Guide for the
Internet Generation

Jill C. Manning, Ph.D.

SHADOW
MOUNTAIN

Visit us at ShadowMountain.com

Library of Congress Cataloging-in-Publication Data

(CIP information on file.)

Printed in the United States of America
Sheridan Books, Inc., Ann Arbor, MI

10   9   8   7   6   5   4   3   2   1

For the young men and women who are striving to be virtuous in a pornography-obsessed society, and for their parents who are striving to teach virtue despite growing opposition

"Both experience and divine wisdom dictate that moral virtue and cleanliness pave the way that leads to strength of character, peace of mind and heart, and happiness in life."

—Gordon B. Hinckley,
Standing for Something, p. 35

Contents

Caution

Reading this book will arm you with truths the pornography industry does not want you to know. Those who believe pornography use can lead to happiness will likely be offended by what is written here and are advised to reread this book after the short-term rush of pornography wears off.

Be advised that the contents of this book may cause increased desire to seek after healthy, well-rounded, and real relationships in your life, as well as give you greater power to resist cheap imitations of true intimacy.

Preface

*"If you can be well without health,
you may be happy without virtue."*

—Edmund Burke

"If what you are saying is true, Jill, why haven't we heard any of this before?" His sixteen-year-old voice was filled with anger, but it was clear he was sincere about wanting to know why he had never heard about the risks of viewing Internet pornography before. The rest of the young men in the adolescent therapy group nodded in agreement with his question.

A shallow or quick response was not going to cut it for these young men, who were smart, computer savvy, and quick to see through sugar-coated answers. In that moment, I realized how ironic it was that these young men had grown up with easy access to pornographic images on the Internet but had had little or no exposure to information about the risks and effects of viewing it. The effects of pornography had literally been censored and hidden from their view during countless helpings of sexually explicit material. This subtle form of censorship had occurred because the effects are not sexually arousing for viewers and therefore are bad for business. Sex may sell, but showing sexually transmitted diseases, addictions, failing relationships, unwanted pregnancies, less than perfect bodies, sexual abuse, and mental illness, tends to have a negative effect on profits. As Shelley Lubben, a former porn star turned activist, states, "Lying is the native language of porn stars because they can't afford to tell you the truth. Not only would it ruin the fantasy for their fans but more important, it would ruin the amount of their paychecks. Don't believe porn actresses when they proudly proclaim they enjoy making porn movies. They're ACTING."[1] In short, the very industry that touts censorship as wrong and un-American has been using a form of censorship and misrepresentation to secure profits.

> Sex may sell, but showing sexually transmitted diseases, addictions, and failing relationships . . . tends to have a negative effect on profits.

Even with this censorship in mind, the young men's lack of awareness about the risks and effects of viewing pornography still seemed odd. Every one of them had experienced negative effects firsthand, including some very serious ones. After all, this was why they were referred to my therapy group in the first place—a group that focused on helping young men learn healthy relationship and coping skills, as well as how to overcome problematic or compulsive sexual behavior. When I stopped to consider, however, that most lawmakers, educators, citizens, and parents do not have a grasp of the full impact Internet pornography is having on the Internet generation, it seemed unrealistic to expect these young men to be aware of the sobering realities of Internet pornography.[2]

The situation reminded me of how the tobacco industry once actively kept the harms of smoking cigarettes hidden from the public in order to make money from the millions of people who were getting addicted to nicotine. The fact that people were dying didn't matter as much as the industry's profits. Now we know the full effect of cigarette smoking and all of the illnesses and deaths it causes. We now know that smoking is directly linked to the top four causes of death in the United States—heart disease, cancer, stroke, and emphysema—and that approximately 400,000 people die every year from smoking-related causes.

Likewise, the young adults who sat in my therapy group had had many important truths about pornography (not to mention healthy sexuality) hidden from them while they got hooked on porn and then developed an appetite for more graphic material. Instead of getting lung cancer, these boys were contracting distorted views about sexuality, bodies, relationships, marriage, men, women, children, and themselves. If these views were not healed or challenged, they would negatively affect their chances of having happy and well-rounded lives. Such views would also impair their ability to achieve healthy, enduring relationships in the future, including a healthy and satisfying sexual relationship.

> Instead of getting lung cancer, these boys were contracting distorted views about sexuality.

These young men were not unique in how pornography was affecting them. What was unique about this group, however, was that someone close to them had recognized how pornography was negatively influencing them and wanted to make sure they got help. Sadly, the vast majority of those who are being affected by Internet pornography are not getting help. They also are not receiving accurate information about this potentially addictive habit and its impact on their futures. To make matters worse, many adults erroneously think Internet pornography is similar to the material that existed when they grew up. These adults dangerously minimize the virtual world of sexual solicitation and hard-core pornography. The time for a wake-up call has passed. We need citizens who are up and ready to do battle against an industry that has been grooming our youth for years. Sadly, much of this grooming has been happening within the confines of our own homes.

The young men in the therapy group viewed pornography as a form of exciting entertainment. It helped satisfy their intense curiosities about sex and provided an easy substitute for the frequently anxious experience of interacting with "real" members of the opposite sex. Pornography, I also learned, had become the cure-all for teenage boredom. *Why* they were so bored in the first place wasn't something they had ever considered. These young men thought of pornography as something normal and common to look at, not to mention increasingly accepted and sometimes even encouraged by the world around them. In fact, many of their male *and* female friends were looking at porn online, which reinforced their view that "porn's okay." As a result, the information I shared with them on that first day of group therapy was a shock to their systems. I had been one of the first people ever to tell them of the negative side of pornography use.

My job as their therapist was to honestly and clearly teach them the information about pornography that had been censored from their view, as well as share with them what a growing number of therapists, physicians, researchers, and religious leaders are finding: that pornography is hindering millions of people from having healthy, happy, and well-rounded lives.

This book is the expanded version of the answer I gave the boys in my therapy group over several months. I hope it meets with their approval and, in the process, helps many others who have questions about pornography but don't know where they can turn for "uncensored" answers.

Please note that I will often refer to the pornography user as "he." This is not to suggest that females don't also have problems with pornography, but it does reflect the fact that the majority of pornography consumers are currently male.

Acknowledgments

Countless books have influenced me, some very deeply. Writing a book, however, has had an even greater impact. Throughout this process, my appreciation and gratitude for the choice people and organizations that have been instrumental in supporting, leading, loving, and teaching me has been heightened and given new meaning.

I am indeed indebted to my beloved husband, Michael; my parents, Fern and Gordon; and my mentors, Dr. Wendy L. Watson and Dr. Alan Parry. I express gratitude to The Heritage Foundation, Senator Sam Brownback and his staff, the National Law Center for Children and Families, Telos Residential Treatment Center, CP80, the LifeSTAR Network, the Utah Coalition Against Pornography, Enough Is Enough, Chris Schoebinger and Jay Parry at Shadow Mountain, my talented colleagues and choice friends, and the young adults who have entrusted me with their stories, struggles, and triumphs. Deepest thanks.

1

What Is Pornography?

"The growth of pornography and its impact on young people is really, really dangerous. And the most dangerous part is that we don't even realize what's happening."

—Pamela Paul

A couple of years ago, a concerned dad took his thirteen-year-old son to a father-son presentation about the effects of pornography. On the drive home, the son turned to his dad and asked, "So, what is pornography anyway?" The dad was floored by his son's question. The two of them had just sat through an hour-long presentation about the effects of pornography, but the son obviously didn't have a clue what the presenter was even talking about. This isn't to say the son had not been exposed to pornography—he had—but he had not made the connection between the *word* pornography and the images that would pop up on his computer screen when he did homework or would play video games online.

Unfortunately, the presenter had assumed that all of the youth in the audience knew what the word *pornography* meant. Because of that false assumption, the much-needed presentation was not as effective as it could have been in reaching and educating youth. It is understandable why the presenter would assume this: the vast majority of young adults in North America have been exposed to pornography or have sought it out themselves. The "pornification" of our culture, to use Pamela Paul's term, has been underway for many years, and just like frogs in a pot of water, we have become desensitized to how many degrees hotter today's popular culture is compared to that of past generations.

To avoid making the same mistake the presenter made, it is important to define the word *pornography* in clear terms. Being clear on what pornography is and how to recognize it is the first step to protecting ourselves.

Pornography Defined

Pornography is material specifically designed to arouse sexual feelings in people by depicting nudity, sexual behavior, or any type of sexual information. This can refer to pictures, stories, sounds, symbols, actions, or words that depict bodies and/or sexual behavior. Pornography can also be created, distributed, and consumed using any type of media. For example, television, radio, books, film, photographs, magazines, cartoons, drawings, videos, DVDs,

CDs, telephones, cell phones, iPods, video games, websites, webcams, and live performances (such as strip clubs) are all ways pornography can be distributed and consumed.

Often young people will tell me something like, "Jill, what I saw wasn't pornography because I didn't get it from a porn shop or website; it was *just* a music video on television." This type of comment reveals a belief that pornography is only pornography if you get it from a certain place or it is presented in a particular way. This is not true! An apple is an apple whether you buy it from a grocery store, pluck it off an apple tree yourself, or have a friend give you one he or she doesn't want to eat. Defining pornography according to where you find it is especially unhelpful in today's world because pornography can be found virtually everywhere, including our homes and schools.

> Pornography is material specifically designed to arouse sexual feelings in people by depicting nudity, sexual behavior, or any type of sexual information.

According to a 2005 study of 718 Swedish high school students from 47 different high school classes, Internet and cable TV were the most common sources of pornography young adults accessed. One of the most shocking findings, however, was that 83 percent of the students watched pornography at home.[3] The trend of people being able to easily access pornography from home is a new phenomenon and, sadly, one that is having very negative effects on their social, spiritual, and sexual development.

> When we see a "dead end" road sign, we do not need to see or experience the terrain beyond the road sign to know that bad things will come from driving ahead.

To help people decide whether what they are viewing is pornography, I encourage them to consider whether a piece of material (such as a music video on TV or an image on a website) causes them to feel sexually excited. Does it cause them to feel like they want to engage in sexual activity or to masturbate? If the answer is yes, it is safe to say that the material is a form of pornography—even if it is not defined as pornography by someone else. Defining pornography for ourselves is an important exercise, and it's one that requires a great deal of honesty.

Warning Signs

When we see a "dead end" road sign, we do not need to see or experience the terrain beyond the road sign to know that bad things will come from driving ahead. Similarly, the word *pornography* in and of itself provides ample warning for us to turn around and completely avoid danger. Additionally, some related words and phrases can be helpful "warning signs" for trouble ahead, and they all deserve the same response—turn around, turn it off, or close your eyes in order to block the sexually explicit material from entering your mind, body, and spirit.

Words and Phrases That Warn Us Pornography Is Straight Ahead

- adult website
- adult bookstore
- porn
- porno
- pornography
- XXX
- Rated R (restricted)
- NC-17 (no one under 17 admitted)
- M (mature)
- AO (adult only)
- sexually explicit material
- peep show
- strip club

- exotic dancers
- adult classified ads
- adult entertainment
- nude show
- topless bar
- escort service
- red-light district
- full-service massage parlor
- cybersex
- phone sex

Trust Your Initial Response

I will never forget the day a kindergarten student was referred to my office for finding pornographic magazines in her brother's bedroom and then taking them to school for show and tell. Can you imagine the kindergarten teacher's shock! The young girl sat across from me and asked, referring to the women in the pornography magazines, "Miss Manning, why do those girls look *so weird?*" This little girl had never even heard of the word pornography, but her question and observation were profound. She knew in her gut that there was something wrong, strange, and unnatural about how the women in the pornographic magazines were being portrayed, and she knew it without any coaching or prodding. In her short five years of life, she had seen enough men and women to know that the women in the pornographic magazines were extremely different and odd when compared to the real people around her.

This little girl's observation reinforced to me that we don't need fancy jargon, legal definitions, or special training to recognize when the human body is being presented in a distorted or unnatural way. Just like Justice Potter Stewart's famous remark about how he would know hard-core pornography when he saw it, I believe everyone can know when something is trying to evoke sexual feelings in them through unhealthy or deceitful means. Confusion sets in only when people start ignoring their gut feelings and start buying into the lies pornography sells. When people accept these lies, they become desensitized to how "weird" this material is and then start rationalizing or justifying why it's okay to look at.

> I believe everyone can know when something is trying to evoke sexual feelings in them through unhealthy or deceitful means.

The little girl's response is pretty typical of what many of us experience when we encounter pornographic material. In describing their own initial response to pornography, people will use a variety of expressions but share similar feelings:

"It grossed me out, but I kept staring at it because it was so bizarre, and I couldn't believe what I was seeing."

"It kind of scared me."

"I felt so embarrassed. I didn't want anyone to know what I had just seen."

"My friends thought the website was really cool. But to be honest, I felt sick inside when I looked at it."

"I felt a rush of excitement, but afterwards I felt guilty because I knew what I had seen was not right."

"I got butterflies in my stomach and felt strange when I looked at it."

"I knew my parents would be disappointed in me if they found out about what I had been looking at."

Being upset or embarrassed are common responses for young people when they encounter pornography online.[4] A 2003 study found that 23 percent of youth were "very" or "extremely upset" by exposure to sexual material.[5] In an Australian study of youth aged eleven to seventeen, the youth often used the words "sick," "yuck," "disgusted," "repulsed," and "upset" to describe how they felt about exposure to online sexual material.[6] So when you feel uncomfortable inside when you encounter pornography, trust your initial response and remember you are not alone.

The Way I See It and Define It

As a therapist who has worked with countless people who have been seriously and negatively impacted by pornography, my view of pornography is understandably different from that of others. I accept that many people disagree with my view, and to be honest, I may have disagreed with it myself before I began working in this area of mental health.

> When you feel uncomfortable inside when you encounter pornography, trust your initial response.

Let me explain how I view pornography so that you will understand why I believe pornography is a very big deal. First, I view pornography as something that is potentially addictive, like a drug. As such, it seriously hinders a person's ability to make clear choices and remain spiritually and physically free. Second, I view pornography as something that can powerfully distort a person's outlook on bodies, relationships, sexuality, and gender. It thereby affects their ability to see life in truthful, helpful, and wholesome ways. I also believe that, due to its distorting influence, pornography undermines opportunities for young people to be self-confident, happy, and to create enduring relationships in the future, including a satisfying sexual relationship with a spouse one day. In short, pornography has become one of the most successfully marketed insults ever made to our humanity, divine nature, and sexuality.

> **Pornography affects all of us even when it is used in secret.**

I have not always viewed pornography this way. Before I became a therapist, pornography was not something I gave much thought to. Although I knew many people had strong feelings about it, I never studied the topic because I never needed to. Further, I didn't really want to know much about it. After all, it seemed like a dark, awful topic. I used to think pornography simply consisted of sexually suggestive or naked photos of women and that people looked at these out of curiosity or loneliness. If someone chose to view pornography, I believed it was none of my business as long as it didn't infringe upon me and didn't hurt anyone—a kind of live-and-let-live attitude.

Nowadays, I know pornography affects *all* of us even when it is used in secret. When someone uses pornography in secret, it changes the way they see the world around them, and this affects everyone who comes into contact with that person. I strongly believe we are all affected by pornography and that the effects are overwhelmingly negative. This is a very big deal to me, and I hope it will become a big deal for you as well.

My First Exposure to Pornography

The first time I encountered pornography was when I was eight years old and in third grade. I was invited to go to my friend Becky's house to play after school. The family room at Becky's house was in the basement, and this is where her board games, dolls, and toys were kept. Unfortunately, that was not all that was kept there. In addition to the games and toys, stacks of magazines lined one wall of the family room. I hadn't paid any attention to the magazines until Becky brought one over to me and opened it up to  the centerfold page. To this day I can recall the image she showed me, even though it was more than twenty-five years ago and I saw it only once. The centerfold image Becky turned to was that of a naked woman with black hair who was lying on a red blanket. My response was one of shock. I had never seen anything like that before and certainly didn't have images or magazines like that in my family room. My next reaction was to feel scared and sick to my stomach. These feelings prompted me to ask where the phone was so I could call my mom and ask her to pick me up. I no longer felt safe or right about being at Becky's house even though she was a nice girl and was fun to play with.

I didn't tell anyone what I had seen at Becky's house, but I felt unsettled for several days and had no desire to return to her house to play. Although I didn't understand at the time why I reacted the way I had, I *knew* there was something wrong about those stacks of magazines and how the woman with the black hair was portrayed. I didn't know what the word *pornography* meant, but I didn't need to in order to know it was wrong.

> When someone uses pornography in secret, it changes the way they see the world around them, and this affects everyone who comes into contact with that person.

When I consider the kinds of images young people today encounter upon their first exposure to pornography, I shudder to think what would have happened to me if I had seen something more graphic at Becky's house. If the centerfold had been more graphic, would I have wanted to see more or gone back to Becky's house again and again? Unfortunately, many youth today are not so lucky when they encounter pornography for the first time. A pornography problem often starts with an innocent curiosity about something seen or heard—and then it can quickly lead to a twisted appetite for more graphic and harmful images.

Daniel's Story

Daniel is sixteen years old and loves karate and working on his Eagle Scout projects. Lately, though, he has appeared down, withdrawn, and tired most of the time. He has become less interested in working on achieving his next karate belt and completing a Scout project he has been excited about for months. What his parents and older siblings don't know is that after everyone is in bed, Daniel has been getting up to watch television late at night for hours at a time. For the last three months, Daniel has become increasingly drawn to some of the latest hip-hop music videos, which show sexually suggestive and oftentimes graphic sexual behavior. When Daniel watches these videos he frequently feels sexually aroused and finds himself daydreaming and fantasizing about what he has seen. He has also begun to imagine what girls at school would look like in such videos. He is watching the music video channel for increasingly longer periods of time without even realizing it. Although Daniel has heard his parents and youth leaders discuss the dangers of Internet pornography, he does not think watching music videos is a problem because it is on television, and everyone in his family has a favorite TV show—music videos just happen to be his favorite thing to watch. When asked about why he is so tired in the morning, he lies and says he just couldn't sleep.

- What are some signs that Daniel is starting to have a serious problem?
- Why does Daniel not make a connection between what he has heard about pornography and what he is doing late at night?
- Do you think Daniel's definition of pornography is helping him or causing him problems? Why?

"I have heard the words soft-core and hard-core pornography. What do these terms mean?"

The terms soft-core and hard-core pornography refer to the degree of nudity and sexual activity that is shown in the pornography. Soft-core pornography is less graphic and detailed. Hard-core pornography, on the other hand, shows everything, leaves nothing to the imagination. Hard-core pornography can also involve violent sexual images or behavior (such as rape). Both soft-core and hard-core pornography can negatively affect people, so it is important to not justify or rationalize frequent viewing of pornography by thinking, "Well, I only look at soft-core pornography, so it's not that bad." All pornographic content has the potential of causing negative effects. It is important to realize that just as using milder drugs can lead to more serious drug use, so soft-core pornography use can lead or escalate to hard-core pornography consumption. Escalation happens as a person craves to see more novel and graphic scenes, and to get a stronger "high."

Definitions of the Different Types of Pornography

Soft-core pornography is less graphic, rarely violent, and does not show detailed images of sexual activity or human genitals. Soft-core pornography can include, but is not limited to, suggestive music videos, swimsuit issues of magazines, sexualized stories, or pictures of partially or fully naked people.

Hard-core pornography is graphic, detailed, and leaves nothing to the imagination. Genitals and sexual activity are shown in detail. Violence is often depicted as part of the sexual activity.

Animated pornography involves cartoons that depict

pornographic stories or images. Some think this kind of pornography is okay because it does not show real people. But it can be just as arousing and graphic as pictures of real people.

Child or "kiddie" pornography is an illegal form of pornography that portrays children or adolescents engaged in sexual activity with other children or adults. This type of pornography is illegal in most countries because it is a form of child abuse. It is extremely harmful to those who view it, as well as those who are used in the production of it.

Bestiality involves sexual images of animals. Bestiality can include images of animals engaged in sexual activity with other animals or humans engaged in sexual activity with animals. This is a very disturbing type of pornography because it shows an unnatural, highly unsafe, and distorted form of sexual activity.

S&M is an abbreviated term for "sadism and

> Just as using milder drugs can lead to more serious drug use, so soft-core pornography use can lead or escalate to hard-core pornography consumption.

masochism," which refers to being sexually aroused by causing mental or physical pain to oneself or someone else. S&M pornography shows images of people being sexually aroused by inflicting pain on someone else or by being hurt themselves. Graphic images of torture are common with this type of pornography.

Gay pornography depicts men sexually engaged with other men or women sexually engaged with other women. Many young people will see this kind of pornography, become sexually aroused by the images, and assume this means they are gay. It's true that some are drawn to gay pornography because they struggle with same-sex attraction, but it is important to remember that most human beings can be aroused by seeing various kinds of sexual behavior. If a person feels aroused by a gay sex scene, this does not necessarily mean he or she is homosexual. There is also a trend to show heterosexual women kissing or making out with one another—the infamous Madonna–Britney Spears public kiss at a music awards ceremony is a mild example of this.

2
What's the Big Deal about Pornography Today?

"We've replaced faith and family with a warped image of sex and self-satisfaction that ridicules the concept of purity and mangles the most sacred ideals of matrimony."

—Ben Shapiro

Pornography is nothing new. In fact, we can find examples of sexually explicit images, statues, and writings dating back to the ancient Roman and Greek empires, as well as early East Indian culture. So, you might ask yourself, "What's the big deal about pornography today?" Well, over the last sixty years, changes in technology and society have dramatically changed the nature of pornography, as well as the pornography industry. It is these changes, along with the ways pornography is affecting individuals, couples, and families, that are causing deep concern.

Today pornography is accepted and glamorized as part of our popular culture. The Internet provides everyone with easy access to the most vile, raunchy, and degrading images available. These are new realities for all of us. As a result, new kinds of discussions and skills are needed to help the Internet generation survive a sex-obsessed culture with their virtue intact. I believe it can be done.

The pornography that people encounter today is disturbingly sinister, graphic, degrading, violent, and distorted compared to pornography of ancient times. In fact, many people would argue that nude or sexual images from ancient times served to celebrate and revere the human body and its potential to create life. As a result, some say, it strengthened a person's desire to take care of his or her body and honor and safeguard sexual intimacy within marriage. This, however, is not the purpose or the effect of the pornography one encounters today. The current plague of pornography is wiping out virtue and making a mockery of the very qualities that make families and societies strong, all the while generating record profits in the process.

> The Internet provides everyone with easy access to the most vile, raunchy, and degrading images available.

Three "Big Deal" Changes

We need to highlight three major changes in society if we hope to explain how and why pornography has become a big deal in today's world:

1. The increase in the volume of pornography
2. The ease of access to pornography
3. The increase in the number of people who are being negatively affected by pornography

Change #1: The Increase in the Volume of Pornography

Consider the following comparisons and calculations that help us understand how much pornography is available in today's world.

- If a young child looked at one new pornographic web page every ten seconds, he or she would be nearly two hundred years old when he or she finished looking at all of the Internet pornography that exists today.[7]
- There are well over 400 million pornographic websites on the Internet. If every pornographic web page was printed and piled up together, the stack of pornography would be over fifteen miles high.[8]
- Every second, $3,075.64 is spent on Internet pornography.[9]

- Every second, 28,258 Internet users are viewing pornography online.[10]
- Every thirty-nine minutes, a new pornography video is produced within the United States.[11]
- As of July 2003, there were 260 million pages of pornography online—an increase of 1,800% since 1998.[12] By the end of 2004, approximately 420 million pages of pornography existed.[13]

Never before has there been so much pornography available. It is almost impossible to keep track of how much is out there because hundreds of new pornographic web pages are added to the World Wide Web each day, and sexually explicit magazines and DVDs are continually being released.

The volume of pornographic material is expected to increase because of the huge profits that are made from selling it around the world, and because it can so easily be created and distributed.

Pornography companies are not the only ones contributing to this increasing volume. Nowadays, virtually anyone can create and distribute pornography through the Internet, digital and web cameras, and cell phones. For instance, by simply taking a digital photograph of someone fully or partially nude and posting it on a website or chatroom site, a person is contributing to the spread and increasing volume of pornographic images. Gone are the days when sexually explicit material is professionally produced only by pornography companies.

> In today's world, it has become almost impossible to avoid pornography completely, but this does not mean efforts to protect ourselves are useless or unimportant.

Because we know that an individual's pornography use often escalates— meaning it increases and gets worse over time—it is expected that the range and types of pornography will continue to expand as people's appetite for more graphic, novel, or strange pornography grows. For those who wish to avoid pornography, it will become increasingly difficult to do so because of the volume and diversity of pornography available, not to mention the increasing number of ways pornography can be encountered. In today's world, it has become almost impossible to avoid pornography completely, but this does not mean efforts to protect ourselves are useless or unimportant. It just means that in addition to making every reasonable effort to avoid pornography, a person must also be prepared to know what to do *when* he or she encounters pornography. This is something we will discuss in chapter 5.

Change #2: The Ease of Access to Pornography

Before the Internet came along, pornography was accessed through restricted movie theaters and bookstores, mail-order catalogs, and select magazine racks. These theaters, stores, and catalogs provided a natural barrier and protection for people who did not want to see pornography. If a person didn't want to be exposed to pornography he or she simply needed to avoid places that sold it. The restrictions on pornography also made it difficult, although not impossible, for youth to access sexually explicit materials because children and adolescents were not permitted in those kinds of stores or theaters.

Never before has the barrier between the home environment and the pornography industry been so thin—and, sadly, in many homes the barrier doesn't exist at all.

Additionally, before the Internet came along, it was impossible for pornography to come into a home, workplace, or school unless someone chose to bring it there. In contrast, today's technologically connected world allows pornography to be streamed, beamed, and dialed into *any* home, school, or workplace even if the recipient wasn't seeking it out. Essentially, if you have access to a television or an Internet connection, you have access to pornography. Never before has the barrier between the home environment and the pornography industry been so thin—and, sadly, in many homes the barrier doesn't exist at all. The ease with which pornography can be accessed by people of all ages is definitely a big-deal change that is affecting our society in profound ways.

Change #3: The Increase in the Number of People Who Are Being Negatively Affected by Pornography

As technology has changed and allowed information to travel around the globe more quickly, pornography has been spread and shared with more people than ever before. Obviously, this means that pornography is now affecting more people than ever before. The reason why this trend is a big deal is that, as I expressed earlier, most of the effects of pornography are destructive and harmful to individuals, couples, families, and society as a whole. And the more pornography spreads, the more these effects will be felt.

Today more than half of the U.S. population use the Internet, which works out to be approximately 172 million people. While the Internet is a very powerful communications and research tool, it is alarming to know that approximately 20 to 33 percent of people who go online use the Internet for sexual purposes—which translates into approximately 34 to 57 million people![14] Just imagine how much good could be done in the world if those same 34 to 57 million people used their computer time to send a kind email to a friend or family member, make an online donation to a charity, get more work done, or look up information about how to make their family, marriage, or life healthier and stronger!

Internet pornography is also more powerful than pornographic images found in print or film because people can (a) choose exactly what they wish to see any time of day and with little or no charge, (b) find images that involve sound and motion, which have a more intense impact on the brain, (c) click through many images in a short period of time and thereby get exposed to more pornography than a magazine or DVD can offer in one sitting, (d) take advantage of what is known as the "Triple-A Engine" effect of *accessibility*, *affordability*, and *anonymity*— meaning the pornography online is easily accessible, often free, and can be sought out without revealing your identity, and (e) become addicted to pornography in shorter periods of time because of the easy access and speed with which they can access large amounts of pornography. So

Internet pornography is not only reaching more people, but it also is having a stronger impact than pornography of previous eras.

But how do we know more people are being affected by pornography? Consider the following points:

- The pornography industry is making record profits. For example, it is estimated that in 2006 the pornography industry generated over $97 billion worldwide, with 13.33 billion of that being made in the U.S.[15] What this means is that the pornography industry is now making more revenue than the top technology companies combined, including Microsoft, Google, Amazon, eBay, Yahoo!, Apple, Netflix, and EarthLink.[16]

- An increasing number of people are seeking treatment for pornography and sexual addictions. According to some experts, approximately 3 to 6 percent of the American adult population is struggling with a sexual addiction (of which pornography use is commonly a part).[17]

- In 2002, the American Academy of Matrimonial (Divorce) Lawyers conducted a survey at their annual meeting in which they asked the lawyers about the impact of Internet use on marriages.[18] The survey indicated that 56 percent of the divorce cases these lawyers handled in the previous year involved one of the partners having an obsessive interest in pornographic websites.

- Fifty percent of the Fortune 500 companies have dealt with a pornography-related problem in their company within the last year.[19]
- In the last ten years, a growing number of anti-pornography and pro-decency groups have formed to tackle the effects and spread of pornography. Groups

The pornography industry is now making more revenue than the top technology companies *combined*, including Microsoft, Google, Amazon, eBay, Yahoo!, Apple, Netflix, and EarthLink.

such as the *National Law Center for Children and Families,* the *Utah Coalition Against Pornography, Enough Is Enough, Communities for Decency,* the *Maryland Coalition Against Pornography,* the *Anti-Pornography League, Cyber Angels,* and *CP80* are just a few of the organizations that are working hard to combat pornography's growing influence. Knowing firsthand how hard volunteers work on these kinds of coalitions and committees, I can assure you these organizations were not created just for the fun of it. They are in existence because of the increased need to speak out and against a growing problem.

· Research journals, such as *Sexual Addiction and Compulsivity: The Journal of Treatment and Prevention,* have come into existence to gather research and address the growing problem of pornography addictions and other compulsive sexual behaviors in society.

> What had started out as an innocent goal of meeting new friends had turned into a very risky situation.

If you have not personally witnessed the growing impact pornography use is having, chances are, you know of someone who has.

Brad's Story

Brad is a fifteen-year-old who uses the Internet on a daily basis to keep in touch with his friends. Because Brad isn't old enough to drive and lives miles away from all of his friends, he has recently been going to chat rooms in order to meet some new friends. One of the chat rooms Brad goes to allows for people to post photos, profiles, and other personal information. Soon after Brad posted a profile on the web, he began getting emails and even phone calls from people he had never met before. He was happy; his plan to expand his circle of friends seemed to be working. After about a month, one of his new "friends" started asking Brad questions about sex and invited him to share very personal and inappropriate information online. Brad felt uncomfortable and wrong about answering, but was scared that if he refused his new friend would make fun of him or stop contacting him.

In time, this so-called friend asked Brad to meet him in person at a mall in a nearby city. Without telling his parents, Brad agreed to the meeting. When Brad showed up, an older man in his forties greeted him and tried to force Brad to leave the mall with him. Fortunately, Brad was strong and fast enough to get away from the stranger and find a phone where he could call his parents for help. What had started out as an innocent goal of meeting new friends had turned into a very risky situation in which Brad could have been kidnapped or abused in some way.

- Where did Brad go wrong, and how did he put himself at risk?
- What are the dangers of meeting new people through the Internet?

• How can a person keep himself safe on the World Wide Web?

> "Why do my parents freak out so much about me meeting people online through chat rooms and websites like MySpace.com?"

I know you may not like to hear this, but your parents have good reason to be concerned about chat rooms and websites like MySpace.com. My guess is that your parents are concerned about your safety first and foremost—even though they may seem controlling and restrictive. For many young adults, chat rooms seem like a safe, fun, and modern way to talk with people from around the world. But this is a risky way to connect socially. Why? Because you can never tell for sure if people are truly who and what they say they are, or what their history is. Unfortunately, it is all too common for adults to pretend to be a child or teen online. Their motive is to trick a real child or teen into a meeting that will result in the youth being hurt, abducted, or sexually abused.

For example, the popular MySpace.com website has more than 180 million profiles, making it the largest social networking site in the world. This may sound like a great way to meet a lot of people. But many sex offenders (people who have been convicted of a sex crime) post profiles on MySpace.com as they seek new victims—even though it is against the law for many of them to use the Internet because of their criminal history. During the first two weeks of May 2007, MySpace.com deleted seven thousand profiles of sex offenders and has removed more since. Sex offenders use MySpace.com so frequently that Ohio's Attorney General, Marc Dann, recently said that MySpace.com is "not a safe environment for children."[20]

> It is all too common for adults to pretend to be a child or teen online. Their motive is to trick a real child or teen into a meeting.

Chat rooms also commonly lead participants into topics and discussions they likely would not have with people in real life. Sex talk, racist slurs, homophobic statements, and sexist and hateful language are commonly found in chat rooms. Going to chat rooms is a little like going to a party where sex addicts, sex predators, criminals, drug dealers, and disrespectful people will be mixed in with the wholesome, clean-cut people. The biggest difference is that

Going to chat rooms is a little like going to a party where sex addicts [and] criminals . . . will be mixed in with the wholesome, clean-cut people. The biggest difference is that at the chat-room "party," every-one looks the same.

at the chat-room "party," everyone looks the same—you can't tell them apart.

Additionally, posting personal information online opens you and your family up to identity theft, sexual solicitation, and the misuse of personal photos and information. I encourage you to get to know real people in real life and then use the Internet (such as email or instant messaging) to stay in contact with real friends. Although the Internet can help people nurture friendships, it is vital to recognize the risks places like chat rooms pose.

3

How Does Pornography Affect People?

"Women became objects to me—sex toys to be used for my own self-gratification. I couldn't walk down a street without imagining what every girl or woman looked like naked. Pornography caused me to become a prisoner within my own mind."

—A twenty-seven-year-old male in recovery from pornography addiction

Do you remember the popular TV show *Friends?* While I am not much of a TV viewer and certainly do not recommend *Friends* as wholesome entertainment for youth, I want to share with you part of an episode that was brought to my attention by a teenage client. The episode is titled "The One with the Free Porn," and it illustrates how pornography affects people's thinking and behavior in a short period of time.

The episode begins with Joey flicking through the channels on his TV and discovering he is able to access a pornography pay-per-view channel free of charge. Out of fear that he and his roommate Chandler will lose this once-in-a-lifetime freebie if they turn the TV off or change the channel, Joey decides to leave the TV running and keeps it fixed on the pornography channel. Through this experience, Joey and Chandler begin to see women differently and begin creating pornographic scenarios out of normal, everyday, and more importantly *nonsexual* events. For example, Joey and Chandler are disappointed when a bank teller and a pizza delivery worker do not want to have sex with them. The episode ends with Joey and Chandler realizing just how twisted their thinking has become from watching the pornography channel and conclude, "Y'know what, we have to turn off the porn!" How I wish more people were coming to the same conclusion.

> Joey and Chandler [realize] just how twisted their thinking has become from watching the pornography channel and conclude, "Y'know what, we have to turn off the porn!"

While this scenario comes from a sitcom on television, the story line of this episode gives a fairly accurate picture of how distorted and unhealthy our thinking and vision of the world can become in a relatively short period of time when we are looking at pornography. Just as Joey and Chandler experienced, pornography consumption causes us to objectify human beings (meaning to treat a person like an object that has no feelings or personality) and view them as sex toys that exist only for our pleasure and gratification. This episode, however, depicts only a few of the ways pornography affects people. Sadly, pornography has many more effects we need to be aware of.

Imagine Your Best Self for a Moment . . . or Better Yet, Forever

When you think of your best self, the person you want to be when you grow up or perhaps be more like next week, what comes to mind? What does that person look like? Act like? Speak like? What kinds of things is he or she involved in? How is he or she making a difference in the world?

Take a moment and list some of the qualities you most want to develop or acquire as you ponder this best self. In order to become this person, what characteristics will be needed? Perhaps you already have these qualities, or maybe they are qualities you admire in your parents, a teacher at school, a youth leader, or even a favorite movie star, biblical hero, historic figure, or athlete.

_____

_____

_____

_____

_____

_____

Now repeat the exercise—but this time list the qualities you most desire in a future boyfriend/girlfriend or
husband/wife.

_____

_____

_____

_____

_____

_____

Now, how would you feel if I told you that using and
viewing pornography will make it almost impossible to
develop or find the characteristics you have just listed? You
may be thinking, "How can you say that when you haven't
seen my list?" Well, assuming you have listed positive traits
and qualities, I can say with a great deal of confidence that
the lists you have created cannot be fostered or developed
fully with pornography in your life, and this also applies to
the lives of those you date and marry. I can say this because

I have come to understand that nothing virtuous or of value comes out of pornography use.

What Research Tells Us about Pornography's Effects

Most of the young adults I meet have limited understanding of the effects of pornography use. But I have observed that young adults typically respond very well to research-based information. They find it a refreshing and useful change from the black-or-white approach they usually experience (pornography is usually presented as a "must see" by friends or a great sin by parents and leaders).

Before we review some of the research findings about pornography use, though, let's look at what research tells us about healthy, long-lasting marriage relationships. This, after all, is the end goal most people have in mind when they start dating or seeking a marriage partner in early adulthood. Most people are not taught enough about what makes relationships or marriages work. By looking at it here, I hope to help you sharpen your relationship skills and highlight how pornography use undermines healthy relationships.

> Nothing virtuous or of value comes out of pornography use.

Characteristics of Stable, Healthy Marriages[21]

1. A mutual belief that marriage is important
2. A mutual belief that marriage is a long-term commitment
3. A mutual belief that spirituality is an important aspect of marriage
4. The ability to be flexible when faced with change
5. Spouses who cooperate and work together
6. Spouses who enjoy spending time together
7. Spouses who feel appreciated and supported
8. Spouses who are faithful and loyal to one another
9. Spouses who use good communication skills
10. Spouses who respect and trust one another
11. Mutual enjoyment of sexual relations that strengthen the marriage relationship
12. An emphasis on positive thinking and acting—positive thoughts and interactions outnumber negative ones with a ratio of 5 to 1 (meaning that for every negative thought or interaction, there are at least five positive ones)
13. Spouses who share similar values

The earlier you can understand and begin to develop the qualities that nurture healthy and lasting relationships, the better your chances will be of being successful in friendships, dating, and family relationships. Learning and striving to apply most of these characteristics early in life will also serve to protect you from pornography's influence. As you review the effects of pornography use, pay close attention to how incongruent and out of sync pornography use is with the characteristics of stable, healthy relationships just listed.

Social science research from the United States, Europe, Canada, and Australia provides the following picture of the effects of regular pornography consumption.[22] Here are twenty-two of the most common effects:

1. Decreased sensitivity toward women—showing more aggression, rudeness, and/or less respect (This happens, in part, because people start to see the women in pornography as objects for their own sexual pleasure rather than as human beings who have thoughts, feelings, choices, family relationships, and needs.)

2. Decreased sensitivity and increased tolerance of sexually graphic material

3. Increased risk of believing rape is not a serious crime or that rape victims are to blame for this type of abuse (This happens when people watch rape scenes in pornography and begin to be aroused by violent, sexual acts, rather than being disturbed or repulsed by them.)

4. Increased risk of being exposed to incorrect information about human sexuality

5. Increased risk of developing unhealthy and

unhelpful views about sexuality (views that do not enhance the health of a person or a relationship)

6. Increased risk of thinking less common sexual practices happen more often than they really do

7. Increased risk of getting involved in sexual behavior that is risky, unhealthy, or illegal (such as hiring prostitutes)

8. Increased risk of experiencing difficulties in intimate relationships

9. Increased risk of becoming aggressive or violent (Sexually violent images have the worst impact on a person's behavior, and nonviolent images have the least impact on aggressive behavior, although they still have a negative effect.)

10. Increased risk of becoming sexually abusive toward others

11. Decreased desire to marry one day

12. Decreased desire to have children and raise a family one day

13. Decreased trust in your boyfriend, girlfriend, or spouse

14. Increased risk of believing long-term relationships are not even realistic

15. Increased risk of becoming sexually dissatisfied with your future spouse

16. Increased risk of cheating on your spouse once you're married

17. Increased risk for separation and divorce once you're married

18. Increased risk of viewing promiscuity or casual sex with many people as normal and natural behavior that has little to no consequences
19. Increased risk of getting fired from your job (if you are looking at pornography at work)
20. Increased risk of believing there is nothing wrong with being sexually active with someone you have no emotional involvement with or commitment to
21. Increased risk of developing a negative body image
22. Increased risk of developing sexually compulsive and/or addictive behavior

As you reviewed this list, I hope you began to appreciate how seriously pornography can influence a person's life and undermine worthy goals and dreams. It

> Regularly think of your best self and who you want to become, making sure your behavior and thoughts are in sync with your goals.

is important that you regularly think of your best self and who you want to become, making sure your behavior and thoughts are in sync with your goals. If you will work hard to avoid pornography or clean it out of your life if you have been viewing it, you will be happier, more successful, and more sexually attractive (and attracted) to your spouse in the future.

> If you will work hard to avoid pornography or clean it out of your life . . . , you will be happier, more successful, and more sexually attractive (and attracted) to your spouse in the future.

Six Effects That Are Especially Important for You to Understand

Six of the items on the above list are particularly important for young adults to consider:

1. Pornography decreases sensitivity toward women.

Pornography encourages people to be less sensitive and respectful toward others because it treats people like objects who simply exist to satisfy another person's sexual urges or desires. The act of treating a person like an object is called *objectification*.

Because the bulk of pornography portrays women as sexual objects, the research commonly discusses decreased sensitivity towards women; however, the pornography viewer can experience decreased sensitivity toward men or children if they are objectified.

Objectification *takes away* human qualities and adds the qualities of an object (something that doesn't speak, doesn't have feelings, and can't make choices) so that people are less likely to relate to, understand, or be sensitive toward the person being shown. Objectification takes place in many ways. Some common ways include covering the face or mouth of a person or only showing parts of a person's body; not giving a person a name or attaching a label that is derogatory or negative; not sharing any identifying information about a person, such as age, interests, family, or education; hiding the true feelings of the person shown so the audience does not know or is misled about how she feels; showing the person in a disrespectful, degrading, or inhumane light; or showing only one aspect of someone's personality or humanity (such as sexuality or the physical body). When humans begin to objectify other humans, we lose part of our humanity and diminish our divine ability to love and care for others.

> When humans begin to objectify other humans, we lose part of our humanity.

2. Pornography encourages distorted and unhealthy views about sexuality.

One of the biggest lies that pornography sells is that viewing pornography will help you understand sexuality better and as a result help you become more confident and "in the know." But here is the truth: *Every* person I have worked with who has been involved with pornography has had less understanding about relationships and sexuality than those who were not looking at pornography. Pornography users have more insecurities around members of the opposite sex and more difficulty in developing close, healthy relationships with people. Pornography provides sexual "mis"-education and is lousy at teaching truth about sexuality and relationships.

When people view pornography regularly they begin to believe some of the following lies:

- Sex is a physical, recreational activity and nothing more.
- Pornography is harmless entertainment.
- Bodies that have been surgically altered (such as through breast or penis enlargement) are more attractive than natural, healthy bodies.
- Having sexual relations with a stranger is more exciting than being intimate with someone you are married to.
- Rape is not a serious crime.
- Sex is the most important part of a relationship.
- Chastity and reserving sexual relations for marriage is unnatural, unrealistic, unhealthy, and old-fashioned.

- It is okay to have sexual relations with children, teenagers, and/or animals.
- Sexual freedom involves acting on sexual impulses whenever you have them and in whatever way you want.
- It is abnormal or strange to not look at pornography.

The last lie I listed is one that is very common for young adults to hear from their peers. Please believe me when I say that there is nothing abnormal or strange about not wanting to expose yourself to degrading, inaccurate, distorting, or illegal information about sexuality. It may be refreshing and extremely mature to not look at pornography, but it is hardly abnormal or weird.

Pornography users who have begun to heal from the distorted beliefs pornography teaches begin to realize how harmful those beliefs are. They begin to see how they limit people

> Every person I have worked with who has been involved with pornography has had less understanding about relationships and sexuality.

from having loving, close relationships. Some of the *truths* recovering pornography users learn and practice living are:

- Healthy sexuality involves intellectual, spiritual, emotional, social, and physical elements. Viewing sexuality as being only physical cuts one off from the full potential and richness of sexual experiences.
- Bodies of all kinds, shapes, and sizes can be sexually attractive if they are well taken care of and treated with respect.
- Having sexual relations with a stranger is risky, unhealthy, and void of intimacy. Meaningful sexual relations take place within the context of a committed relationship and are used to strengthen the bonds between a man and a woman.
- Rape is a horrific crime that is extremely traumatic and one of the worst experiences a human being can experience.
- While sexual relations are an important part of a marital relationship, the emotional, spiritual, social, and intellectual elements of a relationship are also important and enrich intimacy.
- Reserving sex for marriage is a healthy choice and can increase a person's chances of success in school, marriage, and life generally. The more sexual partners a person has prior to marriage, the greater that person's risk of

divorce and of acquiring a sexually transmitted disease.

- Sexual activity with children, teenagers, or animals is abusive, illegal, and unhealthy.
- Sexual freedom is rooted in self-discipline, exercising good boundaries, respecting and protecting one's body and values, and developing a strong character.

3. Pornography causes the viewer to see promiscuity or sexual relations with many people as normal and natural behavior.

While casual sex and promiscuity have become extremely common in the world we live in, the consequences of these behaviors remain unchanged. Today, there is a notion that sexual relations require lots of practice with a wide range of people in order to be enjoyed to the fullest later in life. When we look at the research, however, we learn that people who reserve sexual relations for marriage (1) are *more* satisfied with their future sexual experiences, (2) have little to no risk of sexually transmitted disease and unwanted

> Viewing sexuality as being only physical cuts one off from the full potential and richness of sexual experiences.

pregnancy, and (3) end up having stronger marriages than people who were promiscuous prior to marriage.

If simply learning about sexuality is your goal, there are many excellent resources and people who can answer your questions (even the ones that may be hard to ask) in honest, helpful, and accurate ways. (See the resources section at the back of the book for more information on this.)

4. Pornography increases the risk of experiencing difficulties in serious, intimate relationships.

How I wish you could sit in my office as I speak with couples struggling with pornography use! I am convinced that if you did you would be shocked at how devastating pornography use can be and why I encourage people to avoid it at all costs.

The pornography industry would love for you to think that couples who use pornography enjoy spiced-up love lives and are brimming over with passion, confidence, and happiness. It's true that the couples I work with do have "spiced-up lives." But the spice they live with usually consists of misery, heartache, mistrust, betrayal, insecurity, and plans to separate or divorce. Many people will argue that the reason why pornography has had a negative effect on a couple is that they had a poor relationship to begin with or that one partner was simply too prudish and close minded about pornography or sex. However, in most cases, one of the partners started looking at pornography before the couple even met, and the relationship was described very positively by the other spouse until the pornography use was discovered.

Couples who have used pornography together (such as watching a pornographic film together) commonly experience stress over feelings of competition, insecurity, poor body image, and comparisons. Either way—whether used in secret or as a couple—pornography use creates problems for couples and interferes with true intimacy. Many men even find it difficult to be sexually aroused and attracted to their wives after pornography has been in their life for some time.

> People who reserve sexual relations for marriage . . . are more satisfied with their future sexual experiences.

One of the main reasons why pornography creates difficulties in close relationships is that pornography involves *disconnecting* from "real" life and "real" people. Intimate relationships, on the other hand, involve *connecting* with "real" life and "real" people. In light of this difference, it makes sense why pornography use and intimate relationships don't mix well. It's simply impossible to disconnect and connect at the same time.

5. Pornography decreases job security due to the risk of job loss if a person is looking at pornography at work or staying up so late looking at pornography that he or she is not productive while at work.

If I asked you what you want to be when you grow up, you would likely be able to list one or more career paths that interest you. Imagine working and studying for years to become what you are dreaming of becoming and then getting fired because your boss found you looking at pornography on a work computer or on company time. You may think, "That would never happen to me!" While I am glad you believe this is a far-fetched reality for you, you need to understand that if you choose to use pornography you are putting yourself at risk for this kind of thing to happen— and believe me, it is happening more and more all the time.

> Pornography involves disconnecting from "real" life and "real" people.

Many large companies have begun to enforce Internet abuse policies by firing employees who use pornography on company computers and/or phones. In fact, this is an increasingly common reason why people are fired. And once a person is fired for this reason, it is very difficult for them to find similar work again.

Universities and colleges have also started expelling students who look at pornography on school computers.

So it is not just your dream job that could be at stake—pornography use could actually prevent you from becoming qualified to do what you want to do.

Many people don't understand this. They think their pornography use will have little to no impact on other areas of their life. This simply is not true. Work and school are

> Many people . . . think their pornography use will have no impact on other areas of their life. This simply is not true.

such huge areas of your life that to have them shut down as a result of pornography use will not only be devastating to you and your family, but it can take years to recover from.

6. Pornography desensitizes a person's feelings toward sexually explicit and/or offensive material.

Desensitization is what happens when a person becomes less sensitive to something or someone due to repeated exposures. This occurs because our brains react more strongly to new or novel things. When we have seen something several times, the novelty wears off and the brain doesn't react as strongly as it once did.

When people first begin using pornography, they usually feel a range of intense emotions. Excitement, disgust, shame, anger, guilt, curiosity, and sexual arousal are common reactions. If a person continues to look at pornography, he can quickly become used to the types of images he started out with and crave more graphic and more extreme images or behaviors in order to receive the same rush he initially felt. If this pattern continues, a pornography habit can become a very serious problem and/or addiction.

Ryan's Story

When Ryan was ten years old, a neighborhood friend introduced him to pornography by showing him pictures of naked women in a magazine. Ryan was intrigued and found himself wanting to see more. He had never seen anything like that before and had always wondered what a grown woman looked like naked. For a while, Ryan didn't know where he could find the types of magazines his friend had showed him. Then he heard from guys at school that it was easy to find nude photos of women on the Internet. When Ryan's parents left the house one day, he started searching for pictures of naked women online and was surprised at how easy it was to find them.

Over a period of months and years, Ryan found

himself spending more and more time searching for nude photos online, and his social life and school work began to suffer. He also started exploring other types of photos and video clips. He eventually found the images he had liked early on had become boring and even kind of silly to him. By the time Ryan reached college, he was viewing Internet pornography daily. He would sometimes spend four to six hours at a time looking up new sex videos and chatting about sex with women online. The thought of dating or having a girlfriend seemed like a waste of time to Ryan. In fact, even spending time with guy friends seemed kind of boring compared to looking at pornography.

When Ryan got caught looking at pictures of teenage girls making out with other girls on a university computer, he was expelled from school and required to move in order to continue his education. To make matters worse, he also faced legal consequences for his actions. Ryan blamed the school and felt singled out. After all, most of the guys he knew were looking at porn online, and he didn't see why it was such a big deal.

- In what ways did Ryan experience desensitization?
- In what ways did Ryan's pornography habit escalate?
- Who should have Ryan blamed for being kicked out of school?

- How was pornography use affecting his life and relationships?

> ## "What is masturbation and what does it have to do with pornography?"

Masturbation is defined as touching, stimulating, or rubbing one's own genitals in order to feel sexually aroused and/or experience orgasm. While people can masturbate without looking at pornography, it is rare that a person will watch pornography and not masturbate. The reason is that pornography is designed to activate sexual feelings, and people will then crave to act on those feelings by seeking a sexual release. So, in most cases, pornography use and masturbation go together and at times can become compulsive problems together.

People have various opinions and beliefs about masturbation, and in today's world it is common for masturbation to be spoken of very positively and as a normal, healthy thing to do. Some, however, view masturbation as a misuse of our bodies that conditions a person to think of sexual experiences in self-centered ways, as well as diminishing one's ability to be self-disciplined and chaste before marriage.

Many negative effects can occur when people masturbate to pornography, and these are rarely, if ever, explained to youth. First, when we have a sexual response while looking intensely at an image, the hormones and neurotransmitters that are released in our bodies during the sexual response act a bit like glue, cementing the image in our mind's eye and making it harder to forget. If a person is looking at a distorted, violent, or unnatural portrayal of sexuality, this glue-like quality increases the risk that we will remember the image and be influenced by it for a long time to come.

Second, people can become bonded and attached to the images they see due, in part, to the hormone oxytocin, which is released during sexual response. This hormone is released in the body to help us bond and feel connected to someone else. Oxytocin has other important purposes as well. For example, when a mother nurses a baby, oxytocin is released in the mother's body. While nursing a baby is certainly not a sexual interaction, the hormone oxytocin helps the mother feel bonded and attached to her baby. When a person masturbates to pornography, oxytocin is released, and this encourages one's body and mind to become bonded to the image or *stranger* they are masturbating to. This bonding effect is powerful when activated between a husband and a wife, but when youth are bonding to fantasy images and experiences, it can deeply and negatively affect their ability to be fully attached to their future spouse.

4

Can Pornography Teach Me Things about Sexuality That I Need to Know in the Future?

"I believe that the best defense against bad ideas is better ideas. But now in our culture the problem is that many people make their living by telling lies and spreading bad ideas. The truth is not getting equal time. We need more public media that exists to enliven and enlighten, not to sell."

—Mary Pipher

Many youth have told me they turned to pornography out of curiosity, desiring to know what a sexual term meant or what sex "looked like." Other young adults have shared with me that they turned to pornography because they thought it would show them what members of the opposite sex expected of them, fearing that if they didn't learn what was expected they would feel inadequate in future relationships.

When young people ask me if pornography can teach them important things about sexuality, the answer I give them is simple: "No. It won't and it can't." The truth is that everything human beings need to know about healthy sexuality can be learned without ever looking at pornography—yes, *everything*. In fact, you will have a *better* chance of understanding human sexuality if pornography is never introduced to you because pornography is so distorting and confusing. For example, pornography treats sexuality like a spectator sport, yet healthy sexuality encompasses many amazing aspects of life: our gender, our body, our spirit, our thoughts, our feelings, our desires, our attractions, and many of our most important hopes and dreams.

> Healthy sexuality encompasses many amazing aspects of life: our gender, our body, our spirit, our thoughts, our feelings, our desires, our attractions, and many of our most important hopes and dreams.

Don't mistake: curiosity is a good thing, and so is having questions about sexuality and relationships. But it is critical to clarify *what* you need to know, *when* you need to know it, and *where* to turn to for accurate information. It is also important to keep in mind that how and when we learn about human sexuality depends upon on our culture, religion, family upbringing, values, maturity, gender, and pace of our own physical and emotional development. What this means is that each person will learn about sexuality differently and at a different pace—and there is nothing wrong with this. The important thing is that everyone learn about this part of themselves in the most healthy and truthful way possible.

Your feelings will help you know if you are learning about sexuality from good, accurate sources or not. If you are learning about sexuality in a healthy and truthful manner, you will feel increased understanding, confidence, and peace during and after learning something new. While it can be common to feel awkward, uncomfortable, or surprised when learning about human sexuality, if you are learning accurate information from a trusted and reliable source, you won't want to hide or cover up your learning the same way people who use pornography do. On the other hand, when you are learning about sexuality from inaccurate sources or through pornography, it is common to feel shame, confusion, fear, insecurity, or a need to hide.

Although many young adults think of pornography as an easy and accessible source of sexual education, it is in fact a source of sexual mis-education due to the lies, exaggerations, and distorted views of sexuality it provides.

I have taught human sexuality courses at the university level and have worked with hundreds of people as a marriage and family therapist, including many couples who were struggling with their sexual relationship. With that background, I can tell you that pornography will cause you far more problems than it will ever help you with. One of the reasons for this is that pornography is rooted in *fantasy* rather than the *reality* of loving, healthy relationships or accurate information about our bodies. Only you can determine whether you want your understanding of human sexuality to be rooted in fantasy or reality. If you desire to understand sexuality in an accurate and truthful way, then striving to avoid pornography will be an important choice to make.

> When you are learning about sexuality from inaccurate sources or through pornography, it is common to feel shame, confusion, fear, insecurity, or a need to hide.

What Can Pornography Teach You?

Pornography can and does teach people many things, but its lessons are not truthful, helpful, uplifting, or even useful. For example, pornography does an excellent job at teaching:

> If you desire to understand sexuality in an accurate and truthful way, [strive] to avoid pornography.

1. How to use people for your own gratification.
2. How to focus so much on the physical aspects of sexuality that the spiritual, social, emotional, and relational aspects of sexuality get ignored.
3. How to become desensitized to the beauty of natural, healthy bodies.
4. How to become self-centered.
5. How porn stars behave when they are acting to make money.
6. How to be emotionally disconnected and distant from your future or current spouse.
7. How to be sexually unhappy and dissatisfied.
8. How to be spiritually disconnected and less sensitive to sacred things.

If you decide these are the kinds of things you wish to learn about, you will get a crash course on how to be unhappy, insecure, empty, and lonely—free of charge! If, on the other hand, you wish to learn how to become a healthy, well-rounded, happy, and successful individual, I can confidently state that pornography *cannot* teach you the things you need to know now or in the future.

> If . . . you wish to learn how to become a healthy, well-rounded, happy, and successful individual, I can confidently state that pornography *cannot* teach you the things you need to know.

Some Things You Need to Know That Pornography Cannot Teach You

Because our sexuality is such a fundamental part of life and who we are, it is normal and natural for you to be curious about it and to want to know what you can do to be prepared for a healthy sexual relationship one day. I often tell young adults that if they truly want to understand sexuality and all it can entail for good, they will be taking an important step in the right direction if they learn to recognize pornography as a shallow and misleading representation of the truth.

Our sexual self is a part of who we are, just as our spiritual self or physical self is a part of who we are. As with any part of ourselves, our sexuality holds great potential to enrich life, foster personal growth, and help us fulfill our purpose and potential. In order for us to be sexually healthy and confident, it is important that we nurture our sexual self through: (1) accurate information, (2) good health care and self-care practices, (3) appropriate timing and introduction of new experiences, and (4) exercising healthy boundaries and limits (such as avoiding substances or activities that can harm our body).

Because our sexual self is the only part of who we are that has the potential to create life, it is naturally tied to unique responsibilities and opportunities for serving, growing, and connecting. Unfortunately, in the world we live in people tend to focus more on sexual rights and the satisfying of sexual feelings than the responsibilities and opportunities inherently linked to our sexuality.

> Our sexual self is a part of who we are, just as our spiritual self or physical self is a part of who we are.

Another important part of learning about sexuality is understanding the types of choices, behaviors, and experiences that can have a negative impact on our sexuality. For example, the following problems can have a destructive influence on the development of healthy sexuality:

- Drug and alcohol abuse
- Sexual, physical, and/or emotional abuse
- Obesity
- Eating disorders
- Self-injuring behavior (such as cutting or burning)
- Bullying
- Sexually transmitted diseases
- Untreated medical conditions (such as diabetes, anxiety, or depression)

In addition, the following experiences and circumstances can also have a negative influence on the development of healthy sexuality:

- Growing up in a home where sex is a taboo topic and questions about your body, puberty, and/or sex are not allowed
- Having limited access to accurate information about sexuality
- Engaging in sexual activity before you are emotionally, spiritually, and/or physically ready
- Growing up in an environment that does not celebrate the equal worth of men and women
- Being repeatedly exposed to media images and messages that promote unrealistic body weights, promiscuity, violence, infidelity, and/or unhealthy relationships
- Masturbating to pornographic images
- Viewing violent pornography

If you have experienced or are experiencing any of the items on this list, please seek help. A qualified therapist, family doctor, religious leader, parent, or teacher may be able to assist you in overcoming the problem and healing from any negative effects that may still be affecting you.

Fortunately, many things can help us become sexually mature, healthy, and confident individuals long before we are sexually active. Many youth, however, jump way ahead of themselves and focus so much on having sexual experiences that they miss out on developing the qualities and kind of character that make for fulfilling relationships, including fulfilling sexual relations in marriage. How I wish more people took the time to learn and understand the personal qualities needed for healthy relationships! If more people did, many relationship and sexual problems could be avoided entirely.

Focusing on character building and on developing the characteristics needed for strong relationships would also help young people avoid a great deal of heartache and unhappiness. For example, I have worked with many young adults who believed that engaging in sexual relations was the most important and the best way to learn about sexuality. After becoming sexually active, however, young people commonly regret their decision. In fact, one survey of young adults showed that 77 percent of those who had experienced sexual intercourse wished they had waited longer.[23] This statistic fits with the types of things I commonly hear young adults say after they have become sexually active:

> Focusing on . . . developing the characteristics needed for strong relationships would also help young people avoid a great deal of heartache and unhappiness.

"I regret I didn't wait for someone who really meant a lot to me—like my future wife."

"My sexual experience has tainted my view of sex—I don't think of it as positively as I used to."

"I am so ashamed that I have a sexually transmitted disease. I got genital warts from sleeping around. I wish I had shown more respect for myself and my body."

"I felt pressured to have sex because I was the only virgin out of all of my guy friends. I wish I had been true to myself and not listened to them."

On the flip side, *I have yet to meet someone who waited until they were married to become sexually active who regretted that decision.* If you truly want positive, healthy sexual experiences in the future, please trust me when I say there are far more important lessons and qualities to be focusing on than seeking out sexual experiences and/or pornography.

So what do you need to know about sexuality? Here is a list of things a person needs to do and to become. It is intended to serve as a starting point. I recommend you discuss this list with a parent or trusted adult, and talk about it in conjunction with personal values. You should add to this list if there is something you believe is important that is not listed here. The goal of the list is to encourage you to focus on things you can be working on now to prepare for healthy and satisfying sexual experiences in marriage.

> I have yet to meet someone who waited until they were married to become sexually active who regretted that decision.

1. Learn how to take good care of your body through exercise, proper nutrition, and proper hygiene practices.

Reason: Being physically healthy is important for your overall well-being, including your sexual functioning and attractiveness.

2. Learn how to live a balanced lifestyle that includes relaxation, spirituality, social connection, mental stimulation, and service to others.

Reason: A balanced life increases your attractiveness to other healthy people and communicates to others that you have respect for yourself and a love for life. Learning to balance your life will also help you to put sexuality in perspective and realize that while it is an important part of life, it is not life.

3. Develop self-confidence through setting and achieving wholesome goals, living in sync with your values, exploring your talents, and giving to others.

Reason: Self-confidence is a very attractive quality and increases the likelihood that other self-confident people will be attracted to you. If you have areas of insecurity (as all of us do), simply do your best to work on this area of your life little by little, seeking out ways to master it over time. Self-confidence gives us strength and assurance when facing new situations, including beginning a sexual relationship with our spouse. On the other hand, people who are heavily involved with pornography almost always struggle with self-confidence. Pornography makes it very difficult to be self-confident because when people view degrading and objectifying material, they are immersing themselves in lies—and self-confidence is always diminished by lies. Truth and virtue breed real self-confidence. As you rid your life of this habit, you will feel more self-confident and at peace.

4. Learn to be honest with yourself and others.

Reason: Dishonesty is the kiss of death to relationships, especially in such intimate areas of life as sexual relations. I often ask wives of men who use pornography, "What has been the worst part of all of this?" and they commonly answer, "The lies." Practicing honesty in all sorts of situations will help prepare you to be honest with your intimate partner. When we are dishonest with those we are closest to, especially a spouse, it can take a very long time to restore trust and mend the hurt we've caused.

5. Learn to be a person of integrity. Being a person of integrity means you are true to your word, follow through with promises and commitments, keep confidences, and can be trusted with people's feelings.

Reason: Intimate relationships involve sharing the most vulnerable, private, and special parts of one's self with another person. If we have not learned to handle delicate and important information with great care, we will be prone to hurting our loved ones very deeply. Integrity is also what prevents people from cheating on their boyfriend/girlfriend/husband/wife, viewing pornography secretly, or having inappropriate contact with members of the opposite sex while in a relationship.

6. Set the goal of remaining abstinent before marriage and of reserving sexual relations for the person you are married to.

> Remaining abstinent before marriage gives you the time to develop yourself and prepare emotionally, spiritually, physically, temporally, and socially for a sexual relationship with your spouse.

Reason: Abstinence is the best protection against sexually transmitted diseases and reduces your risk for divorce in the future.[24] Young adults who abstain from sex are also less likely to get involved in delinquent behavior and more likely to do better in school. Remaining abstinent before marriage gives you the time to develop yourself and prepare emotionally, spiritually, physically, temporally, and socially for a sexual relationship with your spouse. Being abstinent also allows you to date more effectively by not getting sideswiped and confused by a sexual attachment to someone who is not right for you.

7. Seek out medically and psychologically sound information about bodies, relationships, and sexual functioning in order to understand sexuality.

Reason: As with any part of life, it is critical to get accurate, high quality information when learning a new subject. Your parents, family doctor, therapist, or youth leader can guide you toward books, websites, or other resources that provide accurate information and can complement what you are learning at home and/or school.

8. Learn what the consequences and responsibilities of sexual activity are.

Reason: It is critical to understand how pregnancy and sexually transmitted diseases affect your life so that you can behave responsibly and avoid causing and/or experiencing a great deal of heartache.

9. Develop your social skills by learning how to interact well with people and how to be comfortable in a variety of social settings.

Reason: Good social skills are an important part of healthy sexuality. Learning to develop these skills at young ages will help you in the future when you are dating, courting, and married to someone of the opposite sex.

10. Develop your spirituality by learning how to nurture your spirit in meaningful ways and by acquiring a spiritual perspective on sexuality.

Reason: In the pornography-obsessed world we live in, gaining a spiritual perspective on sexuality can serve as an anchor. Our relationship with God can also give us strength and encouragement as we strive to develop the qualities that will help us fulfill our full potential.

> Learning to manage sexual feelings and how to use them constructively is part of becoming a mature adult.

11. Develop patience.

Reason: If you are committed to remaining chaste before marriage, you will need patience in order to endure temptations, natural desires, and the ups and downs of dating. Patience will also serve you well in any kind of relationship because it will help you be prepared for the natural pace and timing of how human relationships unfold.

12. Learn that sexual feelings are normal and can help motivate us towards important goals in life (such as dating, marriage, and starting a family), but also learn that they do not need to be acted upon whenever we have them.

Reason: People who regularly look at pornography condition themselves to think and feel that if they have a sexual feeling they automatically need to act on it in some way. This is not true! You will not die by not acting upon all sexual feelings, and in fact, people who act on all of their sexual feelings usually have problems in other areas of their life—such as overeating, impulsive shopping, regular gambling, or drug abuse. Learning to manage sexual feelings and how to use them constructively is part of becoming a mature adult.

> When abusive and traumatic experiences are not healed, people are prone to seek out unhealthy relationships and/or to engage in self-destructive behavior.

13. Seek professional help to resolve and heal any traumatic experiences related to sexual, physical, or emotional abuse in your life.

Reason: When abusive and traumatic experiences are not healed and dealt with in healthy, constructive ways, people are prone to seek out unhealthy relationships and/or to engage in self-destructive behavior due to feelings of shame and self-loathing. Seeking professional help as early in life as possible is an important step in being prepared and open to a healthy relationship in the future. Seeking help will also improve the relationship a survivor of abuse has with himself or herself.

14. Other things you believe you need to know about sexuality, or things you wonder about regarding this subject:

_____

_____

_____

_____

_____

_____

Learning about sexuality and relationships is a normal and necessary part of growing up. Where you turn to for information, however, can make a huge difference in whether or not you develop a healthy and helpful understanding of human sexuality. Identifying accurate and trustworthy sources of information is important—and keep in mind that pornography is not one of these. Parents, teachers, leaders, therapists, doctors, and a variety of books and nonpornographic websites (www.kidshealth.org is an example) can be useful resources to you as you learn about sexuality. Part of our sexual learning includes developing the qualities that are necessary for healthy relationships, as well as identifying the habits, attitudes, and attributes that you can focus on and develop before marriage. Pornography's focus on the physical and carnal aspects of sexuality is a damaging roadblock to understanding healthy sexuality, and nothing that is needed, helpful, or wholesome can be taught by pornography.

Kara's Story

Kara is a seventeen-year-old high school student who has grown up in a home where the subject of sex is taboo and discussions about feelings or sensitive matters are avoided at all costs. Last year, Kara overheard a sexual term being discussed by a group of girls on the bus, and she felt embarrassed and inadequate that she didn't know what the girls were talking about. Later that night, Kara decided to Google the term on the Internet. To her surprise, she had the answer to her question within minutes, but she also got way more than she bargained for! Web page after web page

> Part of our sexual learning includes developing the qualities that are necessary for healthy relationships.

not only described the term she had been so curious about, but also showed men and women engaged in sexual acts. The images were shocking to Kara, but she felt excited and relieved to find such an easy source of information. Kara kept her Internet search a secret and from that point on would Google any term or phrase she heard at school or at the mall. Soon, she was spending more and more time on the computer and started exploring chat rooms where she could discuss her new learning with others. She began to feel like she was "in the know" and "with it" sexually. Her grades at school began to suffer and she also became more withdrawn and less social with young men and women her age.

- Have you ever been curious about sexuality or a sexual term and not known where to turn? What did you do?
- How else could have Kara handled her curiosity?
- What tells you that Kara's choice began to cause problems for her?
- What could Kara's parents do differently?

"Where can I find good information about sex?"

I get asked this question a lot, especially by parents. It is a good question because there is so much incorrect information swirling around us regarding sexuality that it can be hard to identify what is accurate and helpful. What makes the question even more complicated is that each family, parent, or young adult will have a different opinion about what accurate, sound information about sex is. Each family will also have different values about what is appropriate sexual behavior or not.

It is rare to find one resource that suits your tastes and values 100 percent, so you may need to pull from several resources. The following list of books and websites is intended to help you and your parents have meaningful discussions together. However, if you find your parents are unwilling or unable to engage in discussions about sexuality, many of these resources can be helpful for you on your own.

1. *How and When to Tell Your Kids about Sex: A Lifelong Approach to Shaping Your Child's Sexual Character,* by Brenna Jones and Stan Jones.

2. *Ten Talks Parents Must Have with Their Children about Sex and Character,* by Pepper Schwartz and Dominic Cappello.

3. *Kids Ask about Sex: Honest Answers for Every Age,* edited by Melissa R. Cox and the Medical Institute for Sexual Health.

4. *How to Talk with Teens about Love, Relationships and S-E-X: A Guide for Parents,* by Amy G. Miron and Charles D. Miron.

5. *Growing Up: Gospel Answers about Maturation and Sex,* by Brad Wilcox.

6. *How to Talk to Your Child about Sex,* by Linda J. Eyre and Richard M. Eyre.

7. *The "What's Happening to My Body?" Book for Boys,* by Lynda Madaras and Area Madaras.

8. *The "What's Happening to My Body?" Book for Girls,* by Lynda Madaras and Area Madaras.

9. *Sex and Sensibility: The Thinking Parent's Guide to Talking Sense about Sex,* by Deborah M. Roffman.

10. *It's Perfectly Normal: Changing Bodies, Growing Up, Sex and Sexual Health,* by Robie H. Harris.

11. Kids Health (www.kidshealth.org).

12. American Academy of Pediatrics (www.aap.org).

5

What Should I Do If I Am Accidentally Exposed to Pornography?

"The happiness of your life depends upon the quality of your thoughts: therefore, guard accordingly, and take care that you entertain no notions unsuitable to virtue and reasonable nature."

—Marcus Aurelius

In today's media-saturated and technologically connected world, *everybody* is at risk of being accidentally exposed to pornography. Even those who work hard to avoid it through the use of filters and careful media choices can find themselves exposed. So it is not a question about *if* you will encounter pornography but rather *when* you will encounter pornography. How we handle accidental exposures is what will determine the degree to which the pornography will affect us and whether or not a pornography habit will take root.

Having learned from my own accidental exposures, and in working with countless parents and young adults

> It is not a question about *if* you will encounter pornography but rather *when* you will encounter pornography.

who have also dealt with this experience, I have learned there are six things we can do to respond effectively to accidental exposures to pornography:

1. Name it.
2. Cover your eyes and/or ears as quickly as you can.
3. Identify the lie and the opposing truth about sexuality.
4. Tell someone about the exposure as soon as possible.
5. Turn to something positive, uplifting, and wholesome to refocus your mind, body, and spirit.
6. Learn from the experience and identify ways that it might be avoided in the future.

1. Name it.

When you accidentally encounter a pornographic image, it is rare to see a warning label that precedes the encounter. You won't hear an alarm bell or a drum roll or a voice that shouts "in ten seconds you will encounter porn!" Most often it is just *there* before you know what has happened—that's why it is called an accidental exposure.

If there were a warning sound or label of some kind, then it wouldn't be an accidental exposure.

Because pornography can pop up or appear without any prior warning, it is critical that we *name it as pornography* as soon as we can. Like other things in life, giving something a name can be empowering and help us know what we need to do next.

Since pornography is designed to activate sexual feelings in seconds and pull us into the fantasy world it is selling, we need to know in advance what we are going to do—a fire drill of sorts. You could rehearse in advance that when you accidentally encounter pornography, you will say to yourself, preferably out loud, "That's pornography!" You may want to share this fire drill with your parents and/or your friends and even invite them into naming it with you if you are together when it happens.

One young man I worked with said to his father, "Dad, the next time we are in the mall or watching television together, if I run into a pornographic image, I am going to quietly say, 'That's pornography!' and then take action right away. Will you help me to catch and name anything I miss?" Over the next several months, this young man and his father became skilled at naming pornography when they encountered it and would help each other take steps to get away from it as quickly as possible.

2. Cover your eyes and/or ears as quickly as you can.

It only takes three-tenths of a second for an image to enter the eye and start a chain reaction in the body. Because of the speed with which pornography can affect the body through our senses, it is critical that we cover our eyes and/or ears as quickly as we can in order to prevent the image from having a bigger impact on us. Stopping its flow into our eyes or ears will help us to think more clearly and make better choices than if we allow the image to really take hold.

> Stopping its flow into our eyes or ears will help us to think more clearly and make better choices than if we allow the image to really take hold by looking for longer periods of time.

The instruction to cover your eyes and/or ears is literal. When you encounter pornography, cover your eyes and/or cover your ears. Additionally, you may need to turn away, leave the room, shut down the computer, switch the channel or station, walk out of the movie theater, or even run away to get out of the situation and to stop the flow of the pornography coming into your senses. Reducing the amount of time you are exposed to a pornographic image will help lessen its impact and make it easier to get back to feeling normal again more quickly.

3. Identify the lie and the opposing truth about sexuality.

After naming it and stopping the exposure, try to identify the lie the pornographic image was trying to sell you. Then immediately remind yourself of the opposing truth regarding healthy sexuality and true intimacy. This is part of what therapists refer to as "contaminating the fantasy" or "breaking the spell" of the pornographic image. Pornographic images lose their power if we can see through their lies and identify how they were trying to manipulate our feelings.

> Pornographic images lose their power if we can see through their lies and identify how they were trying to manipulate our feelings.

Pornography activates sexual feelings by getting people to believe that what is being shown is sexy and desirable. If people can see through it and recognize, for example, that the porn star is being paid to look that way and behave that way, and that he or she is someone's son or daughter, it can help put the image into a different context for us. Anytime we humanize and personalize the image, it makes using the image for our own self-gratification less appealing.

Because our brains cannot tell the difference between a real or imagined image, we have to help our brain by walking through in our minds what is real and what is not. Again, parents or trusted adults can help you in doing this.

One young man told me that when he would encounter pornography, he would quickly remind himself that the person portrayed in the image was a child of God and not designed to be used as a sex toy for the public. He would also remind himself that the person in the pornography was an individual with thoughts, feelings, and needs who one day would be someone's husband or wife and that only that person's spouse was allowed to see them naked or in a sexual way. The truths in these thoughts helped this young man resist pornography's influence.

4. Tell someone about the exposure as soon as possible.

Problems with pornography are almost always fueled by secrecy and keeping encounters with pornography hidden from others. Secrecy allows the lies of pornography to fester in your mind and remain unchallenged and unchecked by others' views and influence, thereby making the images stronger and more twisted in your mind. Because of the role secrecy plays in the development of pornography addictions, breaking down secrecy is one of the first steps to preventing a serious problem. Telling someone about exposure(s) to pornography early on in your life can provide invaluable protection. I offer this suggestion to adults as well and follow this guideline in my own life. For example, when I accidentally encounter a sexually explicit image, I make a point of telling my husband about what happened the next time we speak by phone or see each other during the day. Doing this helps me release the image from my mind and not allow it to affect my mind or feelings any further.

> Many pornography problems never even get started when people follow the simple rule of telling someone about what they have seen shortly after seeing it.

It can be uncomfortable to tell someone about something we see, but I promise you that doing so will prevent an accidental exposure from becoming a problem that really would be uncomfortable to share. Telling someone is a healthy and mature choice that can make a difference for people of any age.

5. Turn to something positive, uplifting and wholesome to refocus your mind, body, and spirit.

Our brains have an incredible capacity for storing and remembering information and experiences—the good, the bad, and the pornographic. This is great if you are trying to remember something, but it is not helpful if you are trying to forget something. Because our brains cannot vomit bad ideas out like the stomach can vomit out rotten food, we are left to find creative ways of getting rid of images and ideas that have a negative effect on us. One way to do this is to expose our brain to even stronger images that are positive, uplifting, and equally able to stick in our memory. Think of it as arm wrestling for your brain. After encountering a pornographic image, it is important that we find a song, picture, activity, situation, or person that is positive, wholesome, and uplifting that can help wrestle the pornographic thought out of the forefront of our minds.

It can be helpful to think in advance of what music, photographs, movies, poems, activities, or conversations could be turned to when you encounter a sexually explicit image.

6. Learn from the experience and identify any ways that it could be avoided in the future.

After the exposure to pornography is over, it is worthwhile to think about how the accidental exposure occurred and if there was anything that could have been done to prevent it in the first place. Sometimes there won't be anything that could have been done differently—it truly was an accident. However, often there are little things that put us at risk for being exposed. Examples include the time of night you were watching TV, the types of searches you were doing on the Internet, the type or rating of movie you chose to watch, or the kinds of friends you were associating with. Taking time to review if there was anything that put you at risk can be enormously helpful in preventing future exposures.

> After encountering a pornographic image, . . . we [should] find a song, picture, activity, situation, or person . . . that can help wrestle the pornographic thought out of . . . our minds.

Being accidentally exposed to pornography does not

mean you are powerless to do something about it. This chapter has given several approaches and responses you can use. But this list of responses is not meant to be exhaustive. Try to identify other creative approaches that will work for you and brainstorm even more ideas with your family. Working together and being open about what we are seeing in the world around us are powerful tools for preventing pornography problems and maintaining high standards of decency.

Justin's Story

When Justin was eleven years old, he accidentally came across some pornographic magazines his brother had hidden under the mattress in the guest room. Although Justin felt surprised, scared, and curious about the discovery, he kept it a secret because he was afraid he would get in trouble if he told anyone. For months, he avoided the guest bedroom, but the images became something he thought about more and more often. One Saturday afternoon when he found himself home alone, he couldn't stand it any longer and anxiously returned to the room to look at the magazines again. When he got there, the magazines were gone. Justin proceeded to go on an intense scavenger hunt throughout the house, searching for the magazines or any other pornography that was hidden, but he couldn't find any.

When he discovered Internet pornography a few weeks later, he was already primed to want to look at more and more pornography. His curiosity had been piqued by his earlier experiences. To make matters worse, there was no filter on the family computer, and his parents never taught him about the dangers of pornography. By the time he was eighteen years old, he had a compulsive pornography and masturbation habit that had been hidden from everyone in his household. When his mother discovered him acting out to Internet pornography on the family computer, he was deeply embarrassed and felt ashamed and guilty about not telling his parents about what had been going on for several years.

- How could Justin's situation have been avoided through using the steps outlined in this chapter?
- Why do you think Justin got interested in Internet pornography right away?
- How could Justin's parents have helped the situation before it reached the point it did?

"When I have been exposed to pornography, I find it so hard to get the image out of my head. What can I do?"

Because pornography activates such strong emotions and reactions in the body, the brain remembers and recalls those types of images easier than other types of images it encounters. First, know that you are normal when a pornographic image "sticks"—this happens to everyone, and the pornography industry uses this to its advantage when it tries to attract new customers. It "sticks" because of (1) how the images are designed, (2) the sexual feelings and urges in our bodies that get triggered by pornography, and (3) how our brains work.

When we don't like an image we have seen, however, we are not helpless. As mentioned in this chapter, it is extremely useful to talk to someone you trust about what you have seen and to describe to that person how the image affected you. For example, did it scare you? Did it make you feel sick? Did it make you feel sexually aroused? Did it bring up questions about sexuality? Did it remind you of someone you know? Did it cause you to remember something traumatic in your life? Talking it out can help get the image out of your head and into a different zone, where it can be perceived and challenged differently.

Also, it is critical to guide your brain and thoughts toward something that is not only positive and uplifting but also intense and powerful, something strong enough for your brain to take hold of and pay attention to. If you have a song, movie clip, activity, excerpt from a book, or photograph that evokes very strong emotions in you, this could be an excellent thing to turn to when you encounter an image or thought you wish to let go of. Be patient with yourself as you learn this skill; it takes practice to know yourself well enough to understand the types of things you can turn to that will get you focused in a positive and different direction.

> Guide your brain and thoughts toward something that is . . . intense and powerful, something strong enough for your brain to take hold of and pay attention to.

6
What Should I Do If I Can't Stop Looking at Pornography?

"The healthy and strong individual is the one who asks for help when he needs it. Whether he's got an abscess on his knee or in his soul."

—Rona Barrett

When people first dabble in pornography, they are most often unaware of how powerful the pull and addictive nature of pornography can be. As a therapist, it is common for me to hear a young person say something like, "It's just so hard! I try to stop looking at pornography, but the temptation gets so strong and I just cave in." Or, when I work with adults, I regularly hear things like, "What I would give to go back in time and to have never gotten involved with pornography in the first place. It has destroyed everything that really matters to me." What these kinds of comments communicate is how difficult it can be to stop using pornography once a person has developed a habit of turning to it. Even though it can be difficult to stop looking at pornography, that doesn't mean it is impossible.

In most cases, a pornography habit begins when a person is a teenager, although a growing number of people are telling me their habit started in childhood (seven to thirteen years of age is the most common age range for children to start looking at pornography, with girls typically starting later than boys). To make matters worse, most people don't seek help for a pornography problem until they are in their thirties. While seeking help is always a positive move, waiting until you're in your thirties makes the problem even more challenging to fix. It *can* be overcome, but reversing fifteen or more years of practicing a bad habit is no small task. If pornography is in your life, be a good friend to yourself and do your very best to clean the habit out of your life right away. This chapter will help you. But if you have tried to stop looking at pornography several times and have not been able to go more than a few days or weeks without using it, you likely need professional help. Parents, teachers, school counselors, doctors, and/or

> If pornography is in your life, be a good friend to yourself and . . . clean the habit out of your life right away.

religious leaders can help you find someone who is qualified to help.

Suggestions for Overcoming a Pornography Habit

Get Real and Get Out Your Calculator!

Most of us underestimate how many times we have engaged in a negative pattern or habit. For example, a binge eater will think she ate far fewer calories than she actually did, a drug user will think he smoked less pot than he did, the video gamer will think he played for fewer hours than he really did, and the person with a pornography habit will be out of touch with how many times he's used pornography. The more a person feels ashamed and embarrassed about a behavior, the more he will try to minimize how big the problem really is, because it is just too painful to see it clearly. One thing that helps is to get a calculator out and come up with some actual numbers regarding how many times pornography has been used. Depending on the situation, it may also be useful to calculate how many hours have been spent on this habit, or how much money has been spent on pornography.

For example, I'll ask, "How many years has pornography been in your life? About how many times a day or week do you look at it?" We then subtract any periods of time they stayed clean and come up with a total number.

I have never met a person who wasn't shocked at the number we came up with. (Parents tend to be even more shocked.) The total number can give someone a concrete way to put the habit in perspective. It

> Rationalizations help us override our values, good judgment, and best self.

also serves as a wake-up call and motivator to stop.

Here's a contrasting calculation: Select a healthy habit in your life and come up with a similar total for that habit. Then compare the pornography use against the healthy habit.

Identify the Rationalizations You Use to Help Keep Pornography in Your Life

All of us tend to rationalize or justify behaviors we know may not be good for us, but that we like to do anyway. A rationalization is a faulty belief, stretched truth, or flat-out lie we tell ourselves in order to make ourselves feel better about our inappropriate behaviors. Rationalizations help us override our values, good judgment, and best self, and if we use them repeatedly over a long period of time, we end up living beneath our potential and disconnected from who we really are. Some behaviors and rationalizations can be quite harmless, and some are even humorous. For example, my husband, who is physically healthy overall, uses elaborate arguments to defend why eating Cocoa Krispies or Reese's Puffs is the most nutritious breakfast choice for his body! However, when people start rationalizing behaviors or habits that have the potential to be addictive, it becomes a very serious matter. Every pornography user I have met uses multiple rationalizations. Some common rationalizations include:

"I can stop anytime I want to."

"One more time won't hurt."

"It feels good, so how bad can it be?"

"I will stop when I get a girlfriend/start college/have less stress in my life."

"This is natural and normal behavior."

"Everybody is doing it."

"At least I am not into drugs."

"I will just keep it a secret. No one will ever need to know."

"I am just very sexual."

"I deserve a break."

"I am lonely."

"If my girlfriend hadn't broken up with me, I wouldn't need to look at pornography—it's her fault."

I encourage people to identify the rationalizations they use to make them feel better about their pornography use, and then help them to be honest with themselves about how those thoughts are affecting their life. This is a difficult thing to do, because we can become so convinced that our rationalizations are true that we don't see them as lies or stretched truths that we tell ourselves. Recognizing rationalizations, however, can give you warning signals that you are about to go down a path that will lead to more guilt, unhappiness, and problems. When you catch yourself rationalizing, quickly remind yourself of a truth about your situation or how you will feel after you look at pornography.

What are some of the rationalizations you use? Write them below—along with the related truths. Here's an example:

Rationalization: "I can stop looking at pornography anytime I want to."

Truth: "I have tried to stop seven times but always fall back into it. I need help stopping this habit."

_____

_____

_____

_____

_____

Figure Out What Matters Most to You and the Goals That Motivate You

If you truly want to overcome a habit of looking at pornography, you must identify the reasons *why* you want to do so, and what you are giving it up *for*. If you give up a habit without having something to replace it with, it can leave a void in your life that will put you at risk for turning to the habit again. If you have a strong sense of purpose behind why you are giving it up and know what you want to have as a replacement, you are better able to stick to your guns and be successful. If you don't have several strong motivators to stop pornography, you may need to do some careful thinking about who you want to become, and then start developing goals that help you move towards that version of you.

> If you have a strong sense of purpose behind why you are giving [pornography] up, you are better able to stick to your guns and be successful.

Several years ago, I worked with a young man who looked at pornography several times a day. He had no major goals, few friends, and poor relationships with his parents. He was doing so-so in school and had no hobbies other than gaming and surfing the Internet for pornography. I said to him, "You know, I can totally see why you look at pornography. It is the only thing you have going on in your life. Sounds like you need to get a life!" Once he identified two important goals he wanted to focus on, ridding his life of pornography became easier because he had a sense of purpose and meaning for doing so.

What are some reasons for you to stop looking at pornography? In other words, what are some life goals that pornography gets in the way of you achieving?

_____

_____

_____

_____

_____

_____

Identify the Needs Pornography Helps You Meet

Pornography wouldn't be in your life if it didn't do something for you. Overcoming a pornography habit involves learning how to take care of yourself in new ways and making sure you are in a healthy zone as much of the time as possible. Review the following list of needs and try to figure out if pornography helps you meet any of them. Keep in mind that each category could contain many more items—use this list as a tool to get you thinking. Once you identify the need or needs pornography helps you meet, identify several healthy alternatives that will help you get your needs met. The more alternatives you can identify the better.

1. Physical Needs
   - I need pornography to relax when my body gets stressed (alternative: exercise).
   - I need pornography to help me get to sleep at night (alternative: go to bed and get up at the same time every school day, and read a book instead of watching TV before bedtime).

2. Social Needs
   - I feel lonely, and looking at pornography helps me escape from that (alternative: call a friend, join a school club or sports league, or devote time to making friends).

3. Emotional Needs
   - I feel bad about myself, but when I look at pornography, I feel desirable and attractive (alternative: develop self-confidence through setting and achieving a wholesome goal, focus on developing healthy friendships with members of the opposite sex, do something nice for someone that involves you sacrificing your time).

4. Spiritual Needs
    • I feel like God doesn't care about me, and I am angry at how alone I feel. I look at pornography for a quick fix (alternative: talk about your feelings with a religious leader or trusted adult, pray, write in a journal).

> Overcoming a pornography habit involves learning how to take care of yourself in new ways.

What are some of the needs pornography helps you meet? What are some healthy alternatives?

Physical needs

_____

_____

Healthy alternative

_____

_____

Social needs

_____

_____

Healthy alternative

_____

_____

Emotional needs

_____

_____

Healthy alternative

_____

_____

Spiritual needs

_____

_____

Healthy alternative

_____

_____

Other Suggestions for Overcoming a Pornography Habit

1. Identify What Triggers You to Use Pornography

A trigger is anything that kick-starts your desire to look at pornography. Identifying what your triggers are is a key step in figuring out ways to change this unhealthy pattern in your life. People are commonly triggered by boredom, loneliness, anger, sexual arousal, hunger, stress, or tiredness. These triggers are often referred to as

B.L.A.H.S.T. by therapists who work with sexual addictions.[25] Circle which words represent your strongest triggers:

BOREDOM
LONELINESS
ANGER/**A**ROUSAL
HUNGER
STRESS
TIREDNESS

Do you have any other triggers (such as time of day, location, being alone, conflict)? List them below:

_____

_____

_____

_____

_____

_____

2. Tell Someone and Be Accountable to That Person

Secrecy breeds all sorts of trouble for negative and destructive habits in our lives. Telling someone you trust about your problem does several important things: (1) it breaks down the secrecy, (2) it provides you access to possible supports, and (3) it makes you accountable

> Telling someone you trust about your problem . . . breaks down the secrecy, . . . provides you access to possible supports, and . . . makes you accountable to someone else.

to someone else. Once you have told this person that you are struggling with a pornography habit, ask him or her if you can check in on a regular basis (weekly or daily) to let him or her know how you are doing. Give this person permission to ask you about your progress. Because so many young adults are using pornography and think there is nothing wrong with it, I recommend you reach out to an adult who will understand and support your desire to overcome this habit.

3. Connect with "Real" People

Pornography trains us to disconnect from reality and to become immersed in a fantasy world. Part of healing from a pornography habit involves becoming more connected to *real* people. That means working on developing healthy relationships with family and male and female friends. One young man I worked with would spend time with his mom, his sister, or his female friends when he was tempted to use pornography. Spending time with *real* women whom he loved and appreciated helped bring him

back to reality and remember that he wouldn't want someone using those women for their own gratification. If you find yourself in a lot of conflict with others or if you are having difficulty turning to real people, you may want to speak with a school coun-

> Part of healing from a pornography habit involves becoming more connected to real people.

selor or therapist about learning good communication and relationship skills.

4. Take Really Good Care of Yourself

When we take good care of ourselves and strive to have our physical, emotional, social, and spiritual needs met in healthy ways, it helps us stay in a safe and balanced zone. When our needs are being met in healthy ways, we are less likely to turn to destructive behavior or go to extremes in our thinking or actions. Take inventory of your life and figure out how you could improve your wellness in one or two areas. You will feel healthier, more confident, and have less urge to turn to pornography.

5. Shake Up and Clean Up Your Room

Most young adults I work with report that their bedroom is the most common place they look at pornography and/or masturbate. If this is the case for you, clean up your room, rearrange your furniture, add a night light, hang some motivating posters or photographs or quotes up on the wall, and improve the overall feeling and atmosphere of your space. By shaking your bedroom up and getting it more orderly, you will find it easier to get into a different mind-set in your bedroom.

> Exercise of any kind can be an enormously helpful tool for overcoming pornography.

One young man I know pinned a photograph of his family on the ceiling above his bed so that when he felt tempted he would be reminded of the people who loved him and were supporting him as he worked to rid his life of pornography. Be creative and have fun with this idea. If you commonly act out in another space, such as the bathroom, take the idea and apply it to that room.

6. Get Busy and Get Active!

Being active and engaged in fun activities is good for your body, mind, and spirit. Exercise of any kind can be an enormously helpful tool for overcoming pornography. Exercise can help you relax, sleep better, feel more confident, and release physical and sexual tension. It will also get you out in the land of the living instead of in front of a computer screen or video game monitor.

7. Cut Down on Sugar and Caffeine

Pornography acts like a stimulant to the body. When you are trying to overcome the temptation to look at pornography, extra stimulants in your body will make it harder to be calm, levelheaded, and able to use your best judgment. Reducing sugar and caffeine in your diet can help with this. One young woman I met noticed a dramatic difference in her ability to fight temptations after she quit drinking caffeinated energy drinks and cut back on her favorite candy snacks. This suggestion will have positive effects on other areas of your life as well.

> Extra stimulants in your body will make it harder to be calm, levelheaded, and able to use your best judgment.

8. Cut Off the Access to Pornography

This is probably the most obvious and simplistic suggestion, but one that a surprising number of people don't take action on. If Internet pornography is a problem for you, shut down your access to that type of pornography. This may involve moving the computer to an open space in your home, having your parents' password protect your computer, installing an Internet filter, using the computers at school or the library for homework, removing Internet access from your home, or temporarily getting rid of your computer all together. Be clear on what is a need versus a want. Your well-being is a need; having easy access to the Internet is a want and a convenience.

9. Establish New Media Standards for Yourself

When you are ridding your life of pornography, it is useful to reevaluate your standards with all forms of media. This may be the time to commit yourself to seeing films of only certain ratings (perhaps PG and below), stop viewing certain television programs, watch TV only during certain hours of the day (for example, before 8 P.M.), delete certain songs from your iPod, and get rid of video games or delete Internet links that have caused problems for you in the past. Set high standards for yourself with the media you are exposed to—what you take in has a significant effect on you.

10. Limit Video Game Use

In my experience, most young adults who struggle with pornography use are also heavily into video games. Limiting video game playing and changing the games you play is often a necessary step in overcoming pornography. The main concerns I have with video games are (1) many video games contain pornographic themes or content, (2) online video games frequently have pornographic pop-ups or ads linked to the game sites, (3) video game playing often becomes excessive and helps young people avoid exercise and well-rounded relationships with others, and (4) video game use helps young people tune out and become disconnected from feelings, conversation, and real interactions for long periods of time. While nothing is wrong with video games in and of themselves, it is important to choose games that are clean and wholesome and to have healthy limits on your gaming so that other areas of your life do not suffer.

> While nothing is wrong with video games in and of themselves, . . . have healthy limits on your gaming so that other areas of your life do not suffer.

11. Learn Something New That's Challenging to Do

Pornography conditions the brain to think and respond in certain ways. Learning something new that challenges and stimulates your brain in different ways can help move powerful associations in your brain out of center stage in your mind. Learning a new language, starting a new hobby, or taking a class to learn a new sport or musical instrument are examples of the types of things that can stimulate the brain in healthy ways. The key is that it has to be something you feel passionate about and feel pumped up about doing.

What are some things you have always wanted to do, try, or learn but haven't yet? List them below.

_____

_____

_____

_____

_____

_____

12. Take Charge of Your Day

The triggers to turn to pornography almost always come when we have let our guard down and forgotten to take care of ourselves in an important way (for example, we have allowed ourselves to get too hungry, too stressed, too bored, or too lonely). Planning your day and making sure your needs get met are important steps in healing. If planning what you are going to do and eat each day seems like too much, start out with a weekly plan of what you need to do in order to remain in a healthy mindset. A day planner, PDA, online calendar (perhaps through your email provider), or cell phone can help you. You may also wish to order Cor-Cards from www.lifestarnetwork.org/bookstore. cfm. These are small daily planners that can fit in your pocket; they have a positive affirmation on the back that relates to overcoming pornography.

13. Avoid Being Alone

When people look at pornography or masturbate, they are almost always alone (if they do it in public, they can be legally charged with indecent exposure or sexual harassment). If being alone is a key trigger for you to look at pornography and you don't trust yourself when you are by yourself, take action to reduce the amount of time you are alone. You can try many things to make sure you are not alone for too long:

> Planning your day and making sure your needs get met are important steps in healing.

ask someone to be with you, leave the bathroom door open slightly when you are in there, remove the door from the entryway to your bedroom, leave the door open if you are just hanging out in your room, sleep somewhere else in the house, share a room with someone, hang out more in rooms in your house where family are more likely to be, or change your sleep schedule to coincide better with that of your parents or siblings.

14. Learn about Human Sexuality from Accurate Sources

Because pornography teaches so many lies about human sexuality, women, men, bodies, and relationships, people who have looked at a lot of pornography almost always have very distorted and inaccurate views of sexuality. Further, pornography users often think pornography is a reliable source of information about sexuality. It is therefore important to reach out to someone you trust (such as a parent, grandparent, religious leader, teacher, therapist, or doctor) to get direction on where you can turn for accurate and healthy information. Even if pornography is not a problem for you, seeking out accurate sources for information about human sexuality is an important part of our development and well-being.

15. Develop Your Spirituality

Pornography separates and disconnects us from spiritual things and everything that is sacred, wholesome, and good. This disconnection is part of the reason why most addiction programs, such as Alcoholics Anonymous (AA), focus on recommitting to spirituality and learning to rely on God or a Higher Power. Recommitting to spirituality helps us become grounded in what our limits and abilities are, what is real and what is false, and how to nourish parts of ourselves that have been neglected or damaged through a destructive habit or addiction. You don't have to be associated with a religion to develop spirituality, although a religious life can help many people

> Recommitting to spirituality helps us become grounded in . . . what is real and what is false.

with this process. Spending time in nature; learning how to pray; learning how to meditate; taking time to ponder, breathe, reflect, or think; listening to sacred music or hymns; attending religious services; reading scripture or holy texts; getting involved in charitable projects or causes; or listening to sermons by religious leaders are all ways that we can nourish our spirit.

16. Serve and Focus on Others

Pornography use breeds selfishness more than any other behavior or habit I know of. Getting over yourself and learning to give of your time, talents, and energy to others are critical parts of overcoming this habit. One

> You will . . . benefit [from] jotting down feelings, ideas, goals, or thoughts about what is going on in your life.

young man accepted the challenge to focus on others by committing to make a daily effort to help his mother around the house, ask how she was doing, and keep his room clean because he knew that was important to her. Not only did his relationship with his mother improve (within days), but he also began to appreciate his mother and other women more. He also began to realize how pornography had pulled him away from seeing the true beauty in real women.

17. Journal Feelings

Writing out our feelings and thoughts is a helpful way to get a different perspective on our life or to just let things out. One young woman who agreed to journal her feelings at least twice a week soon realized how much sadness she felt and how sadness was a trigger for her to turn to sexual chat rooms online. Even if you use a journal only for a short period of time, you will likely find benefit in jotting down feelings, ideas, goals, or thoughts about what is going on in your life.

18. Ride the Wave Out

Those who have developed a habit of masturbating to pornography often develop the belief that if they feel a sexual urge or feeling they must act on it right away. Learning to ride those feelings out without acting on them is an important step in recovery and self-discipline; therapists often refer to that step as "riding the wave out." People are often surprised to learn that nothing bad happens when they acknowledge the urge but don't act on it. In the same way that self-discipline is the key to a healthy life with regard to eating, sleeping, and managing emotions, learning to manage sexual feelings (and realizing that we may have such feelings without it being appropriate to act on them) is a sign of maturity.

19. Join a Support Group

Group therapy and support groups can be extremely effective in helping people overcome compulsive sexual behaviors such as masturbation and pornography use. Many high schools and universities offer a range of support groups for young adults, and an increasing number of therapists offer groups that deal with pornography specifically. The *Life*STAR Network, for example, offers therapeutic groups for adults and adolescents dealing with compulsive sexual behaviors (www.lifestarnetwork.org).

20. Seek Professional Help from a Therapist Who Treats Pornography Problems

As mentioned before, if you have tried several times to stop looking at pornography and have been unsuccessful in doing so, please consider getting professional help from someone who specializes in pornography addiction or problematic sexual behaviors. You can look in the yellow pages under psychologists, counselors, or marriage and family therapists; then look for someone who works with sexual addictions. Just as not all medical doctors are trained to treat all medical problems, not all therapists are trained to work with pornography problems, so be sure to find someone who can help in this specific area of your life. Finding a specialist will ensure that you get the best care possible and that you don't spend more time in therapy than you need to. The earlier you can reach out for qualified help, the easier it will be to overcome this.

21. Talk with Your Doctor

Some people struggle with a medical problem that makes it more difficult for them to overcome a pornography habit. Conditions such as anxiety disorders, attention deficit disorder (ADD), attention deficit and hyperactivity disorder (ADHD), depression, obsessive-compulsive disorder (OCD), eating disorders, and sleep disorders are examples of the types of medical problems that can make it more difficult to stop looking at pornography. If you suffer from any of these conditions, please see your medical doctor right away. Even if you don't have a medical condition that is complicating your recovery, it may be useful for a medical doctor to prescribe medication if you are being compulsive (out of control) in your behavior and having great difficulty stopping something. Many of my clients report good success when they have combined therapy and self-help with medical intervention. Explore your options and circumstances with your doctor if you think this could be something that may help you succeed.

22. Practice, Practice, Practice!

Overcoming any habit takes hard work and patience, not to mention *practice, practice, practice*. If you have identified some strategies that you think will help you in your goal to be free of pornography, be patient with yourself as you learn to master these new skills. Often pornography problems remain hidden and secret for a long time before people get help or even decide that they need to stop; in the same way, it can take a while for new habits to take hold. Celebrate the fact that you are even willing to address this issue in your life and then do your best. When you get stuck or have slips, reach out for help and support. You do not have to tackle this issue on your own.

23. Learn the Truth about Pornography Stars

When I share truths about the pornography industry and the pornography stars who perform in pornography, most people experience a radical shift in their perception and attitude. If you have never given the truth about pornography stars much thought, you may want to watch the documentary *Traffic Control: The People's War on Internet Porn* (www.trafficcontrolthemovie.com), in which a former male and female porn star share their story of working in the industry. Because most people who use pornography have certain beliefs about the porn stars in order to feel okay about objectifying them and using them for their own gratification, it can be therapeutic to learn the truth about what really is going on for a porn star. Some of the beliefs that commonly get challenged or changed include: porn stars enjoy what they do and experience pleasure while acting, porn stars are just very sexual people, porn stars desire me, and porn stars are the kind of people I would love to know

> The goal is . . . to replace the [pornography] habit with healthy practices and attitudes towards sexuality, life, relationships, and yourself.

in real life. As you contemplate your beliefs about porn stars, consider the following points:

- The majority of pornography stars have been victims of physical and sexual abuse.
- Most struggle with drug addictions and are on drugs when they perform.
- Most feel unworthy of being loved.
- Most deal with mental health issues (such as post-traumatic stress disorder, depression, personality disorders, or extremely poor self-esteem).
- Most endure emotional and physical pain, not pleasure, while performing in pornographic scenes (a common reason why so many get high or stoned before performing).

When we begin to think of pornography stars as real people who are sisters, daughters, brothers, sons, mothers, fathers, and friends who have names, needs, feelings, and often a tragic personal history, we can break down the objectification that is used to keep them locked in a fantasy world for our selfish purposes.

24. Other Ideas for Overcoming a Pornography Habit

_____

_____

_____

_____

_____

_____

Overcoming a pornography habit is hard work, but it is possible. The approaches people use to overcome a pornography habit usually need to become part of their lifestyle if they hope to stay safe and healthy over the long haul. Because of pornography's influence on the brain, some of its triggers and associations will always remain in your memory and can put you at risk for acting out again. The goal is to stop pornography from being an active problem and to replace the habit with healthy practices and attitudes. By applying the suggestions in this chapter, along with your own creative efforts, you can develop a winning combination for ridding your life of pornography's influence.

Amanda's Story

Amanda is a twenty-one-year-old who works part-time in a popular clothing store and is attending college at the community college near her home. She used to be very outgoing and social, but since her boyfriend broke up with her a year and a half ago, she has become more withdrawn and isolated. When the breakup came, she was naturally sad and upset, but instead of talking to friends and family about her feelings, she escaped into online chat rooms and discussion groups that focused on breakups and dating. After about a month of using chat rooms, she began checking out pornography websites that were designed for young women. She felt temporary relief from her depression as she fantasized about the young men who were shown online. Her habit of escaping into the fantasy worlds of pornography and chat rooms only got worse as her depression was left untreated and her old friends slowly stopped calling her.

Amanda's wake-up call came when a man with whom she had flirted in a chat room suggested that they meet in person to have sex. Amanda got scared and realized how distorted her life had become and how far away from her values she had strayed. She finally talked to her parents and asked for their help in protecting her from online sexual solicitation, as well as in breaking her pornography habit.

- How did Amanda become vulnerable to pornography?
- What were the risks to Amanda's safety if she had gone to meet the stranger?

- What different choices and coping skills could Amanda have used after her breakup?
- What would you have done if you had been Amanda's friend?
- What could Amanda's parents have done before this situation became so serious?

"I found some pornography on the family computer and I think it belongs to my dad. What should I do?"

Discovering that your parent is using pornography can be very upsetting. Many youth I have worked with were afraid they would get in trouble for squealing if they told anyone about their parent's pornography use, or that they would be accused of trying to blame someone else for their own pornography use. It is okay to take some time to think about how to best approach this problem. The important thing is to talk to someone who can help you take action in some way.

If you have a good relationship with the parent you suspect is using pornography, try to bring it to his attention and describe how it made you feel inside to stumble upon what you did. If you are somewhat distant from this parent or feel scared about bringing it up, do your best to find another adult you can talk it through with. For example, you may feel comfortable speaking with your other parent, an aunt or uncle, a grandparent, a church leader, a doctor, a therapist, or a close adult friend. Hopefully, this other adult can help you brainstorm some ways of handling the situation or could even step in to help the parent themselves. The important thing is that you get some support and talk it out with someone. Keeping it a secret can be damaging both to you and to your family. Also, it is not considered squealing when we sincerely want to help someone (or ourselves) and are unsure of how to handle a tough situation that is negatively affecting us.

> It is not considered squealing when we sincerely want to help someone and are unsure of how to handle a tough situation.

What Should I Do If I Know Someone Who Can't Stop Looking at Pornography?

"Example is contagious behavior."
—Charles Reade

It is unsettling to learn that someone we know is viewing pornography. Feelings of mistrust, hurt, concern, anger, fear, confusion, and uncertainty are common. Sometimes the toughest thing of all can be realizing that there are limits to what we can do to help someone and that ultimately that person is the only one who is fully responsible and able to stop viewing pornography. Despite the limits on what we can do to help another person, there are still some things we can and ought to do when possible.

What Are the Signs Someone Is Using Pornography?

Unlike drug use or other types of destructive behavior, pornography use can be difficult to detect—there are no sure-fire ways to tell if someone is using pornography. It is even more difficult to detect if the individual is working hard to hide his pornography use from others. The following list of common symptoms and signs can be helpful, however. As you review this list, keep in mind that some of these symptoms can be signs of other problems, such as depression, anxiety, or being a victim of bullying. Don't jump to conclusions regarding pornography use if a person you care for is exhibiting some or all of these signs.

> Pornography use can be difficult to detect—there are no sure-fire ways to tell if someone is using pornography.

Common Signs and Symptoms of Pornography Use

- Withdrawing from friends and family
- Spending increased time alone
- Staying up late at night
- Experiencing increased fatigue (due to changes in sleep schedules)
- Experiencing decreased concentration
- Showing increased moodiness and irritability
- Making unusual or unexplained purchases or financial transactions

- Spending increased time on the computer
- Experiencing decreased performance at school or in sports
- Showing decreased sensitivity to sacred things and topics
- Manifesting increased aggression and disrespectful attitudes towards others
- Manifesting a negative change in attitude
- Developing a pattern of lying
- Using vulgar language and/or references to sexual terms that seem out of character
- Making disrespectful or irreverent comments about sexuality and/or relationships
- Looking at and becoming fixated on people's body parts rather than their face
- Manifesting changes in sexual behavior
- Becoming anxious or angry when someone walks into the room while he or she is on the computer
- Deleting the history cache on the computer after he or she uses the computer
- Spending unusual amounts of time at the public library or at another person's house
- Having decreased desire to attend religious meetings
- Making negative comments about marriage or having a family one day that are out of character
- Losing a job suddenly
- Having unexplained debts

- Being expelled from a university
- Having decreased self-confidence

What Should You Do If You Are Not Sure If a Person Is Involved in Pornography?

If you suspect someone has a pornography problem but don't know for sure, there are a few things you can do. Keep in mind, though, that if someone really wants to hide his pornography use, he can, and if he really does not want to change, we are limited in our influence. Parents who suspect a child is involved in pornography have more power to intervene (for example, they can install filters, arrange therapy, clarify and enforce house rules, teach healthy sexuality and Internet safety, or support a child who is actively trying to overcome it), but even parents face limits in their ability to stop someone else's behavior.

> If someone really wants to hide his pornography use, he can, and if he really does not want to change, we are limited in our influence.

If you fear someone else has a pornography problem, ask yourself how well you know him and how he will respond to a very personal question about a very sensitive subject coming from you. How you approach a very close friend or family member is going to be different from how you approach a classmate you don't know very well. One thing that can be helpful is to imagine how you would feel if this individual came up and asked you if you are looking at pornography. If it would seem rude and totally out of line, you may want to reconsider how specific you should be.

Even if you do not know the person well, you can still offer a general observation about something you have noticed and share a general statement of concern. For example, you could say, "(Name), I know we don't know each other well, but I have noticed you just seem kind of down lately. I hope you are okay. If there is anything I can do for you, please let me know."

You can also express your concern to a trusted adult who does have a relationship with the person you are concerned about—or at least has some power to influence him (such as a teacher, church leader, coach, or parent). To this adult, you could say something like, "I have been very concerned about (name), and fear he/she may be involved in pornography. Because I know you have a good relationship with him/her, I thought you would know better than I about how this could be handled. May I leave this concern with you?" You may want to ask the adult to keep your involvement confidential.

If you do have a personal relationship with the person you are concerned about, then talking with them directly makes sense, but you will still need to prepare your thoughts and questions in advance, in order to be as clear, calm, and helpful as possible. Identify the behaviors, symptoms, or feelings that are causing you concern. The more specific you can be the better; you need to be prepared to answer his questions if he acts confused about what you **are** talking about or denies anything is wrong. For example, you may prepare in advance to note that the four things that concern you most are: (1) how withdrawn he has become over the last (month/year), (2) the dramatic increase in the amount of time he is spending on the computer, (3) the crude, sexual humor he now uses, and (4) any specific incident where you discovered pornography on his computer or witnessed him viewing pornography.

After you are clear on what your concerns involve, write out or think through what you want to say and what questions you want to ask. You will then need to choose a time and private place to share what you have prepared. Think through what you would like to see happen as a result of your conversation. Do you want to just talk to him and confirm or dispel your concerns? Do you want him to take some sort of action? Or do you want him to just know you have noticed a change in him?

For example, suppose I am worried that my brother is looking at pornography. I may choose to go to his room on a Sunday afternoon when everyone is taking a nap and say something like, "(Name), for about the last two months, I have been really worried about you. The things that have worried me the most are that you spend more and more time on the computer, you seem down a lot, and you have seemed less interested in things you usually love to do. I really miss your old self, and I am wondering if pornography is having a negative influence on you, or if there is something else I should understand. If there is anything I can do to be of help, I would be very happy to do it."

If the person you are concerned about responds positively and begins to open up, be sure to give him your very best listening ear. Also, have in mind an idea or possible resource to offer him when he is finished talking (for instance, the name of an adult he could speak with for help, the name of a book that could help him—there are some in the resources section at the back of this book—or reassurance that the two of you will work on a plan together).

If he does not respond positively or shuts down and gets defensive, don't push the matter. Instead, simply emphasize that you are concerned and willing to talk or help in the future if he so desires. If you haven't already spoken with an adult who is close to this person, now would be a good time to do so. Share your feelings of concern and what you've done to reach out.

If approaching an individual directly does not feel like the right thing to do, you could make a point of simply bringing up the issue of pornography and expressing your feelings about the *issue* rather than your concerns about the *person*. For example:

- One young man was worried about his brother. He decided that during a family dinner he would share an interesting fact about pornography use with his family and use that fact as a way to open up the subject to his whole family for discussion. No one person was singled out, but it did get the topic out in the open.
- A young woman sensed that her younger brother was looking at pornography. She privately urged her parents to install a filter on the family computer and to lead a family discussion about Internet safety.
- Another young man encouraged his family to watch the DVD *Pornography the Great Lie: A Guide for Families of All Faiths* as a family activity.
- One mother decided to watch the movie *Traffic Control: The People's War on Internet Porn* (www.trafficcontrolthemovie.com) with her

family and discuss pornography as a social issue as a family.

- Another young woman who had concerns for her older brother (who worked in the computer industry) asked him, "I know pornography use can be an issue for people who work a lot on computers. How do you keep yourself safe from that kind of material?"

> There are many creative and wise ways the issue of pornography may be raised.

What these examples demonstrate is that there are many creative and wise ways the issue of pornography may be raised if speaking with someone directly is not an option or not something you feel comfortable doing. Parents, on the other hand, are encouraged to be more bold and direct in their approaches, considering the devastating effect pornography can have on a young person, as well as the home overall.

What Should You Do If You Know for Sure Someone Is Involved in Pornography?

Because people generally try to keep their use of pornography a secret, they often have a great deal of shame and defensiveness when they are questioned about it. If you think you should talk to someone you are certain is using pornography, take time to prepare your thoughts. Identify the solution or outcome you would like to see happen (for example, you could ask him to meet with a trained therapist, clergy, or parent).

Healing from a pornography habit involves removing or breaking down the secrecy around it. But breaking down the secrecy can be very threatening for the person who is trying so hard to keep it a secret. Nevertheless, some pornography users will feel relieved when someone else brings it up and does the secret breaking for them. Others will get scared and even angry.

> Healing from a pornography habit involves removing or breaking down the secrecy around it.

They may need some time after the issue is raised in order to calm down and get in a frame of mind where they can listen to your concerns or ideas.

The following list provides some ideas of what you can do when you know someone is using pornography. Keep in mind that this list is not exhaustive. It is also important to be considerate of the unique ways a particular individual may be best approached.

- Let the person know you are aware he is using pornography.
- Clearly state your concern and fears.
- Ask if he wants help to stop this habit. If not, why not?
- Be patient. Just because you are ready to talk about this problem, doesn't mean he will be. You may need to try again at a later time.
- Use a section from a book, article, DVD, or quote to refer to if you need some backup as to why this is a problem and/or what can be done about it.
- Offer suggestions about possible boundaries that could help him stop viewing pornography (such as removing the computer from his bedroom, having someone else set up the passwords on the computer, installing a filter that specifically blocks sexually explicit content, limiting time alone, getting involved in a sport after school, and so forth).
- Encourage him to speak with someone who is trained in how to overcome pornography habits and addictions, and have specific names and phone numbers ready. Offer to be willing to go with him if he is afraid to go alone. *Professional help is especially needed if he has tried to stop several times and has been unable to stop.*
- Encourage him to become accountable to someone else, meaning he will share with

someone else on a daily or weekly basis how
he is doing.

- Suggest wholesome activities, such as sports,
  clubs, service projects, spiritual practices, or
  goals that could be substituted for pornography use. Be willing to do some of these with
  him.
- Offer to learn more about the effects of pornography use and how to overcome it
  together.
- Be positive and encouraging. Pornography can
  be very difficult to get out of one's life, so you
  will need to be patient and realistic. If you
  expect him to immediately stop looking at
  pornography, he may feel intense guilt and
  shame if he slips, and he may worry that he
  can't be honest with you because he will dis-
  appoint you. Feelings of shame and guilt can
  also trigger many people into wanting to look
  at pornography to escape from their pain.
- Ask how pornography meets his needs, and
  then brainstorm ways those needs could be
  met in healthier ways.
- Ask what triggers his pornography use: boredom, loneliness, anger, sexual arousal, stress,
  or feeling tired? Brainstorm ways these triggers
  can be avoided and handled differently.
- Keep confidences. Don't tell others what this
  person is going through. If you do, he will lose
  trust in you. Of course, telling a trusted adult

is encouraged if you are the only one who is aware of the problem, but once help is put in place, don't be a gossip.

What If the Person You Are Dating Is Looking at Pornography?

Young people often ask me what they should do if someone they are dating is using pornography. This is a tough question to answer because it is never my place to tell people who they should date, or under what circumstances they should date. Nevertheless, I strongly believe that pornography pollutes a dating relationship. A breakup should be seriously considered if the pornography use is not dealt with and stopped right away. This may sound harsh, but a breakup can serve as a wake-up call to the pornography user that his pornography problem needs to be dealt with. A breakup can also prevent the nonuser from getting further into a relationship that will cause a great deal of heartache—or much worse (for example, date rape, a future marriage that is polluted with pornography and ends in divorce, or experiencing disrespect from one's partner because his attitudes have been affected by pornography). Taking a firm and clear stance against pornography shows a great deal of self-respect and communicates to your friend that he or she is not living up to his or her potential and your expectations of a dating partner.

I can't count the number of people I have worked with who have said, "Jill, I wish I had taken this problem much more seriously when we were dating" or "I just thought this was something everybody did. I had no clue about how damaging it would be to our relationship and my self-esteem" or "I thought it was my fault and therefore my job to fix it. I now realize it was 100 percent his problem—and while I was trying to fix it, I missed out on dating some really great people." Please, please, please, if you are dating someone who is using pornography, take this issue very seriously. Think very carefully about the consequences of remaining in a relationship with a pornography user.

> Taking a firm and clear stance against pornography shows a great deal of self-respect.

If you are okay with a boyfriend or girlfriend using pornography and it is not a big deal for you, I encourage you to explore why this is the case. Taking pornography lightly often reflects a lack of accurate information, lack of self-confidence, or unresolved past issues. Consider: What are your beliefs regarding pornography use and its effects? Do you use pornography yourself and therefore don't feel like you can question someone else's pornography use? Do you lack self-confidence and don't believe you deserve a healthy relationship in which you are treated with respect and fidelity? Do you know of another dating relationship in which pornography use occurred and you believe it did no harm?

Most young people ask me about dating and pornography because they want to know how to "fix it" or find out what they can do to stop their boyfriend or girlfriend from using it. They think that if they just try harder or use the right approach, all will be well. They want to be the hero or heroine that saves the day and rescues their friend from the evil dragon called Pornography. While this heroic attitude is admirable, it can often lead a young person deeper into a dating relationship that is unhealthy and on very shaky ground. It can be hard for these eager individuals to hear that no one can *make* a person stop looking at pornography—it is an individual choice that can be influenced but not forced.

Surprisingly, some pornography users blame their partners. To do so is simply to fail to take responsibility for one's own actions. On the other hand, some nonusing partners will commonly blame themselves. In their lack of self-confidence, nonusers may think that if they were prettier, better looking, smarter, more athletic, and so forth, their partner wouldn't be turning to pornography. This is a lie!

Sometimes young people treat dating like marriage

and act as if they must continue to date at all costs because that is what committed, romantic people do. But the purpose of dating is to learn how to interact with members of the opposite sex, have fun, learn the qualities in people you find attractive and unattractive, and begin to understand what kind of person would be a good marriage partner for you in the future. Too often, people will let their feelings make all their decisions for them, and they remain in a dating relationship that is unhealthy or even abusive because they are scared of what would happen if they broke up. Or they are determined that this is who they are going to marry one day, so they need to suck it up and live with the problems no matter what. Please be cautious of making premature commitments to someone you are dating and not married to.

If you are dating someone who is using pornography and it is upsetting for you, express your concerns. If your boyfriend or girlfriend does not immediately take your concerns seriously and commit to stop looking at pornography, please consider a breakup. Pornography is too degrading and destructive to mess around with. Pornography use is not simply a pet peeve; it is a destructive influence that can seriously damage a person's life. If you express your concerns and your boyfriend or girlfriend commits to stop and seems to follow through, go slow, but remain on your guard.

The Limits around What You Can Do

By now, you have probably realized that making someone stop looking at pornography is not within your power. We cannot make anyone change but ourselves. However, it is within our power to influence, be an example, support, encourage, offer ideas, express concern, pray, communicate expectations, set boundaries, and make changes ourselves.

It takes enormous courage to stand up and say to someone that pornography use is not acceptable to you or that you are concerned for someone. However, as we try our best to ensure that our homes, friendships, relationships, and lives are free from the destructive influence of pornography, we will be happier, more confident, and more at peace.

> We cannot make anyone change but ourselves.

It is also important to remember you are not alone. Millions of others are battling this issue, and there are an increasing number of resources for people of all ages to take strength from. Do what you can and do your best at it, and I promise good will come of it—for you and for those within your circle of influence.

Kevin's Story

Kevin is a fifteen-year-old young man who lives with his parents and three siblings. For the last three years, Kevin has secretly been viewing pornography on the Internet. Because of the pressures he was facing at school, he gradually started to turn to pornography more and more. His mother noticed that Kevin had become more withdrawn, depressed, and began to have difficulty in school, and she suspected something was not right. After speaking with the school counselor, Kevin's mother decided to install a software program onto the family computer that allowed her to secretly monitor what Kevin was looking at online and when he was doing so. Through monitoring his Internet activities for three weeks, Kevin's parents learned that he was going to pornography websites at least five to six times a week and was spending up to four hours on the computer each time. They decided to sit down with him after his younger siblings had gone to bed and express their concerns to him. They first expressed their love and concern for him, but they also made it clear that pornography use was not acceptable in their home and would need to stop. Kevin's dad had researched resources in the city where they lived, so they could offer Kevin some options about how he could get help in stopping his behavior. Kevin was defensive and deeply embarrassed, but deep down he also felt relieved that he could get some help. He had been feeling bad about himself and had tried to stop many times. Within two weeks, Kevin was participating in a teen pornography group that helped give him helpful tools to cope with stress, boredom, and his emotions. The group also gave him specific tools he could use to overcome his pornography habit. Although Kevin and his parents got into fights while he was overcoming his pornography habit, he slowly became more open with his mom and dad and they started relating to him better than they had for some time. They also began to trust him more as he showed through his actions that he was making progress and was using the Internet responsibly.

- How did Kevin's parents prepare to speak with him?
- How do you think Kevin and his parents felt during the conversation when his pornography use was brought up?
- What would have happened if Kevin's mom had not acted on her concerns or had ignored the problem?
- Why do you think Kevin felt relieved?

"How can I tell if pornography is a problem for me or not?"

If you are wondering if pornography is a problem for you or not, consider how you would answer the following questions. If you answer yes to any of the questions, please seriously consider seeking professional help.

1. Do you ever spend more time than you had planned on looking at pornography?
2. Do you spend more time looking at pornography than you did when you first started to look at it?
3. Has your school work or job suffered as a result of your pornography use?
4. Have any of your relationships with family and/or friends gotten worse since this habit started?
5. Have you noticed any changes in your mood or self-confidence since you began looking at pornography?
6. Do you have difficulty concentrating on things you need to because you have thoughts and fantasies about pornography on your mind?
7. Do you find it hard to stop looking at pornography even when you really want to?

8. Has anyone ever forced you to view pornography?
9. Have you ever been sexually abused and find yourself turning to pornography as a way to make sense of your trauma?
10. Do you spend more time alone than you used to?
11. Have you ever lied to cover up your pornography use?
12. Do you regularly turn to pornography for information about sex?
13. Have you ever stolen money or used someone else's credit card to purchase pornography?
14. Do you have difficulty sleeping as a result of your pornography use (meaning, because you stay up too late surfing the web)?
15. Do you have increased difficulty interacting with members of the opposite sex?
16. Do you find yourself aroused by sexual images involving violence, animals, or children?

8

12 Suggestions for Parents

"A little knowledge that acts is worth infinitely more than much knowledge that is idle."

—Kahlil Gibran

The Internet has changed parenting. Protecting children from pornography, online sexual solicitation, and virtual bullying have become new realities for today's parents. These new realities, however, have also brought forth new opportunities for teaching sexuality and fostering emotional intelligence more effectively. And they have helped us learn how to prepare our children to be safe in a virtual world that is increasingly necessary for them to know how to function in.

Like any generation of parents, it takes us time and resources to understand how to adapt to new realities. Fortunately, an increasing number of excellent resources are available for parents and educators to use. The following twelve suggestions are intended to provide parents with suggestions for tackling many of the issues addressed in this book. These suggestions are rooted in clinical work with adolescents, pornography-related research, and the work of various coalitions and organizations committed to protecting decency and combating the effects of pornography.

1. Be Aware . . . Be Very Aware

Parents who grew up in the pre-Internet era often have a hard time comprehending the full scope of dangers and risks their children are exposed to in the virtual world. The first step to protecting one's family from the risks of Internet pornography and other online dangers (such as virtual bullying, sexual solicitation, sex predators, identity theft, and harassment) is to be aware that these are happening online. Online resources such as those listed in the resources section can be an invaluable way to learn about the virtual world in an efficient and inexpensive manner, as well as get help in teaching your whole family about Internet safety.

> Like any generation of parents, it takes us time . . . to understand how to adapt to new realities.

Parents also need to understand that the pornography of today is very different from the material that existed when they grew up. Internet pornography is easily *accessible* from your home, *affordable*, and can be viewed *anonymously*. These unique features of the online world, which are commonly known as the "Triple-A Effect,"[26] provide a drastically different scenario from the days when people had to purchase pornography from XXX stores in seedy areas of town or order it through catalogs that came wrapped in brown paper.

Internet pornography also differs from print and film material in that it is highly interactive (people can search for exactly what they want to see, when they want to see it), and it stimulates more senses due

> The pornography of today is very different from the material that existed when [today's parents] grew up.

to the sound and movement that accompanies most websites. Additionally, the Internet provides almost immediate access to some of the worst, most vile, and obscene material that exists. Learning to be aware of what our children face in the virtual world is critical if we hope to help guide and navigate them through terrain that has unprecedented risks as well as unprecedented opportunities for learning and connecting to the world around them.

2. Understand How Youth Access Pornography

The Top 8 Ways Young Adults Tell Me They Have Accessed Pornography

1. Using Internet websites and downloads
2. Watching television late at night
3. Watching movies that show explicit sexual activity
4. Watching music videos (It is no accident that music videos were referred to as "beginner's porn" during a 2007 television special on CNN's *Paula Zahn Now.*)
5. Viewing postings on MySpace.com or other social networking websites
6. Playing video games that have pornographic themes or have hidden pornographic scenes within them
7. Receiving cell phone downloads
8. Finding or being given a pornography magazine by a friend or older sibling

> Internet pornography is easily accessible from your home, affordable, and can be viewed anonymously.

In theory, pornography was never intended for children and adolescents, and that is why it is often referred to as "adult" content or material (even though it isn't good for any age group). Research shows, however, that an increasing number of children and adolescents have access to pornography and that pornographers often target youth with misleading domain names, pop-ups, or web advertis-

> Pornographers often target youth with misleading domain names, pop-ups, or web advertising.

ing. While it is illegal for pornographers to distribute pornography to minors, our society has been inexcusably slow to enforce these laws.

The reason why minors' access to pornography has been limited by law in the past is that children and adolescents are considered the most vulnerable audience of sexually explicit material—in other words, they are the group most at risk to be negatively affected by pornography. Youth are considered a vulnerable audience because they (a) can be easily forced into viewing pornography or used to make pornography, (b) have difficulty understanding sexually explicit material, (c) can easily be harmed by someone else's pornography use (especially by a parent or sibling), (d) can have their sexual and social development negatively affected through exposure to the lies pornography promotes about sexuality and relationships, and (e) can develop unrealistic expectations about their future sexual relationship with a spouse.[27] For these reasons, it is illegal to distribute obscene material to minors.

Unfortunately, the number of children and adolescents exposed to these risks is increasing as young people start using the Internet at younger ages and get online more frequently. For example, in 1998, 4.1 percent of three- to four-year-olds, 16.8 percent of five- to nine-year-olds, and 39.9 percent of fourteen- to seventeen-year-olds regularly used the Internet. By 2001, however, the numbers had jumped to 14.3 percent for three- to four-year-olds, 38.9 percent for five- to nine-year-olds, and 75.6 percent for fourteen- to seventeen-year-olds.[28] Of course, not everyone using the Internet is looking at pornography. But the more time people spend online, the more they are at risk for accidentally encountering sexually explicit material. A 2002 study, for example, found that 70 percent of youth ages fifteen to seventeen reported accidentally coming across pornography online, and 23 percent of those youth said this happens "very" or "somewhat" often.[29] On the other hand, if a person is actively searching for Internet pornography, he or she will find material easily. Only 3 percent of pornographic websites require proof of age before granting access to sexually explicit material,[30] and two-thirds of pornographic websites do not include adult content warnings.[31]

While we know that the easy and free access youth have to pornography is a new phenomenon in our society, we are less certain what the consequences will be in the long term as the "Internet Generation" grows up and starts marriages and families of their own. The trends and statistics we have so far do not paint a positive picture of the effects, nor of what is to come, and this is a major reason why easy and free access to pornography is a big deal.

3. Be on the Offensive

The pornography industry is doing everything it can to make money and increase its consumer base. One way it does this is by playing hardball online through the use of pop-ups, web ads, farcical age-verification systems on pornographic websites, and misleading domain names. Pornography was the very first industry to make money online, and it monopolized this first-place position for many years. In short, this industry knows what it is doing; please don't underestimate it. The fact that a growing number of youth are exposed and targeted means nothing more than future profits to this industry. As a result, parents need to be actively protecting their families and homes from Internet pornography. When a parent says to me, "But I trust my child to not look at Internet pornography," my reply is, "Regardless of how well you trust your child, never trust the pornography industry or the sexual predators online." We also know from research that almost half of the youth who are sexually solicited online do not tell anyone about it, and few who encounter upsetting material online ever tell someone. [32] What this means is that parents can easily underestimate the negative or risky experiences their children are having online.

> Pornography was the very first industry to make money online, and it monopolized this first-place position for many years.

Please be wise about what your children, and what we as parents, are up against. Some of the things a parent can do to protect and prepare their children include:

- Teaching Internet safety in the home
- Setting media guidelines for the home and modeling the use of wholesome entertainment
- Installing computer filters
- Placing family computers in open spaces of the home
- Teaching healthy sexuality early and in a layered fashion

A growing number of resources can assist parents in following through with these steps (see the resources at the back of the book). By taking active steps, parents can help safeguard the well-being and normal social and sexual development of youth within the virtual world.

4. Teach Healthy Sexuality Early and Layer the Discussion throughout a Child's Development

Gone is the day of the one-time sex talk. Today, children and young adults are exposed to sexual information at earlier ages than previous generations, and our parenting strategies with regard to sexual education have not kept up to their modern-day reality. Despite the highly sexualized and confusing world young adults live in, parents often remain reluctant to discuss sexual topics with their children[33]—a dynamic that heightens the confusion as well as the appeal of pornography.

I will never forget working with a young man who said to me, "Jill, I began looking at homosexual pornography at the age of ten and by the time my parents talked to me about sexual intercourse at age thirteen, I was convinced they had no clue what they were talking about! I had come to learn that homosexual sex was sex, period." Sadly, this young man's parents offered too little too late.

It is important that parents take center stage early in a

child's sexual development and become a clear, bold, honest, and loving voice that can provide a buffer and reference point against the lies their children encounter. It is disturbing to learn that some experts in the field of communications believe sexualized media have become the primary agents of sexual socialization for our youth.[34] Parents can take encouragement, however, in knowing that studies have shown that young adults prefer to receive information about sexuality from their parents.[35]

> Despite the highly sexualized and confusing world young adults live in, parents often remain reluctant to discuss sexual topics with their children.

My colleagues and I advise parents to start teaching human sexuality in early childhood and then to layer and expand the discussion over the course of the child's development. Many parents are locked into thinking that sexual education should focus solely on sexual intercourse and should commence either right before or sometime during puberty. This is simply not true, not to mention very outdated for the reality our children face at school, in the media, and online.

Effective sexual education encompasses a range of topics that can be addressed at various ages, with the age of two being a good launching point. Sexual education can comprise discussion and training related to the difference between inappropriate and appropriate touch, respect and care for the body, anatomically correct names for parts of the body, honesty, trust, identifying and managing emotions, how to deal with stress and conflict in healthy ways, how to be a good friend to yourself and others, boundaries, sexual abuse prevention, assertiveness, respect for yourself and others, communication skills, puberty, abstinence, sexual intercourse, masturbation, healthy versus unhealthy relationships, birth control, sexually transmitted diseases, pornography, pregnancy, and family values (particularly those relating to premarital sex, dating, and abortion). As we learn to blend sexual education into a child's development, our children are more likely to identify fraudulent messages about sexuality and have a greater chance of becoming healthy, confident individuals.

> Parents [must] take center stage early in a child's sexual development.

5. Carefully Place, Monitor, and Filter Family Computers

Placing computers with Internet access in children's bedrooms is asking for trouble when it comes to pornography and online dangers. Alternatively, keeping computers in open areas of the home, such as a family room, study, or kitchen is easy to do and can prevent a host of secretive and risky behaviors. Additionally, installing a computer filter on family computers can help limit inappropriate content from coming into the home, especially if you have young children in your household. Websites such as www .internet-filter-review.com can help parents select a filter that is right for their needs and budget.

> Keeping computers in open areas of the home . . . is easy to do and can prevent a host of secretive and risky behaviors.

But filters must not be viewed as a long-term solution or complete defense. Computer-savvy youth can disable filters or work around them with relative ease. The clean port technology initiative that the CP80 group (www.cp80.org) has proposed and is working hard to get implemented on a wide scale will one day offer a superior solution to filters, but for now filters are the best we have for reducing the risk of exposure.

Ironically, the use of filters works against needed legislation because the pornography industry and even the courts argue that because parents can install filters, there is no need to regulate sexually explicit material or to restructure the Internet. I have lost count of how many young adults have come to me with pornography problems who had filters on their home computers! While an important preventative measure for younger children, filters are not a solid solution when young adults are in the home. The best defenses we have right now include filters combined with active parenting, careful placement of computers, the setting of media standards, and the teaching of Internet safety and healthy

> The best defenses we have right now include filters combined with active parenting, careful placement of computers, the setting of media standards, and the teaching of Internet safety and healthy sexuality.

sexuality. Even though filters are not perfect, I encourage parents to use everything at their disposal.

6. Clarify Media Standards in the Home and Model Wholesome Consumption of Media

In order to set media standards in the home, parents need to agree between themselves what the standards should be and how to go about implementing them. If children receive the message that the media standards apply to everyone in the home and that the parents are modeling wholesome media selections themselves, the children are more likely to understand and abide by the standards set. In a lot of families, parents assume that the media standards are known and understood by the children, even though nothing has been clearly stated or discussed. Engaging in open discussion and family planning sessions regarding media standards, as well as clearly stating or writing out what the standards are, is very helpful. Websites such as www.pauseparentplay.org can

> Children [must] receive the message that the media standards apply to everyone in the home.

help parents and families with these kinds of decisions and discussions.

7. Discuss the Issue of Pornography

In the same way that secrecy is the breeding ground of pornography problems, open, frank discussion about the dangers of pornography and a parent's stance on it can prevent problems from developing. Because people commonly become exposed to pornography between the ages of seven and thirteen, we should discuss pornography early and in age-appropriate ways, all the while putting in place protections on family computers and other media outlets. The talking points found on pages 166–68, as well as at the end of each of the personal stories found at the end of each chapter, are intended to spark and guide this very kind of discussion.

8. Teach Internet Safety

When I was growing up, kids received lessons at home and at school about the importance of not talking to strangers and what to do if a stranger offered them candy or tried to give them a ride home from school. Today, playgrounds, parks, and public spaces are not the most dangerous places for a child—unfiltered, unmonitored Internet use is. When a child logs on to the Internet he or she literally surfs, searches, and communicates within the same virtual space that sex predators, pedophiles, criminals, and pornographers use. Although millions of exceptional people are also using the Internet, they are seldom the ones your child will meet online. Teaching Internet safety has become the new "must-have-talk" with kids. Topics of discussion may include the importance of not sharing personal information online (such as address, phone number, school, full name, photographs, and so forth); how to shut a computer down; how to do effective searches online; the need to get Mom or Dad if someone speaks inappropriately with them or asks to meet them in person; how to identify pornography; and email etiquette. There are many resources available for parents, and many of them are free to use online. See the resources section at the back of the book for recommendations related to Internet safety in the home.

> Although millions of exceptional people are also using the Internet, they are seldom the ones your child will meet online.

9. Use Parental Controls

There are diverse types of parental controls that can help families limit their exposure to sexually explicit material in the media. Televisions, DVD players, computers, video game modules, and satellite radio are all forms of media that can be managed to some extent through the use of parental controls. For those who are not technologically savvy and who may feel intimidated or unsure about how to activate or use parental controls, the *Pause, Parent, Play* organization (www.pauseparentplay.org) can be a tremendous resource. *Pause, Parent, Play* provides simplified instructions for using parental controls as well as links to various companies that do the same.

10. Model Healthy Stress and Emotion Management

Most people who struggle with a pornography habit have a hard time identifying and coping with emotions and stress in constructive ways. When children learn early in life how to manage emotions well, their ability to creatively deal with stress and emotional situations later in life is greatly enhanced. Anger, sadness, loneliness, stress,

> When parents model how to express and use feelings to make healthy decisions, a child has an important leg up.

and fear are common emotions that people struggle with. When parents model how to express and use feelings to make healthy decisions, a child has an important leg up in this area of emotional development. Parents can help foster emotional well-being in a variety of ways, but some that have been especially useful in my work with families have included:

- Spotlight one feeling each week for a period of time and discuss that feeling as a family over meals or in conversations. Discussions may include how the feeling can be identified in others or in yourself, what kinds of events may trigger that feeling, creative ways to use or deal with that feeling, and times when each family member has felt it.
- Select children's books that highlight or focus on feelings and read them together.
- Play the *Ungame* card game as a family (www.EducationalLearningGames.com).
- While watching movies as a family, take time to highlight emotions that the characters are experiencing and whether the character is coping with that feeling well or not.
- Create or find a lengthy list of feelings and use the list to do personal inventories with one another about how each person is feeling.
- Play emotions tic-tac-toe. Create a tic-tac-toe matrix. Then write a feeling word in each box of the matrix: angry, happy, sad, lonely, stressed, surprised, frustrated, relaxed, tired (the order

does not matter); include feelings that family members have felt recently. Enter a total of nine feelings. Using pieces of wrapped hard candy (one kind or color per player) as your game pieces, each player tries to get three game pieces in a row (vertically, horizontally, or diagonally) on the matrix. Each time an individual places a game piece on a square, however, he must share an example of when he felt that way recently. The first person to get candy on three squares in a row wins. The pieces of candy may be shared at the end of the game.

angry	happy	sad
lonely	stressed	surprised
frustrated	relaxed	tired

- Select a variety of songs that can be played on a CD player. After playing each song, discuss what the emotional tone of each song is and why each person arrived at the answers he or she did.
- Take time to check in with one another about how each of you have felt that day and what each of you did to deal with the feeling.

11. Get Professional Help When Needed

If a person has attempted to stop looking at pornography several times and has been unable to, professional and specialized help should probably be sought. Psychologists, marriage and family therapists, licensed counselors, social workers, clergy, or psychiatrists who have training dealing with addictive or compulsive behavior, pornography, or Internet addictions can be helpful with this kind of problem. As with any type of professional service, be a wise consumer. Before proceeding with a particular specialist, be sure to ask about his or her approach, views on pornography, training, and how open he or she would be to respecting your family's religious beliefs and values. The resources section can help you seek out a professional who works with pornography problems or problematic sexual behavior.

> Often people find it helpful and even therapeutic to support, join, or become involved in such groups, especially if they have felt helpless with regard to a loved one's problem with pornography.

12. Support Prodecency Efforts in Your School, Community, and State

A growing number of organizations and coalitions are striving to protect youth from pornography's influence, as well as to raise the standard of decency in our communities. Often people find it helpful and even therapeutic to support, join, or become involved in such groups, especially if they have felt helpless with regard to a loved one's problem with pornography. Involvement in a community, state, or national organization is often recommended after one's own immediate struggle or family crisis has passed, although getting involved right away can be empowering for some and offer a needed positive distraction. Many people report that getting involved in a prodecency or antipornography coalition helps them channel their anger, frustration, or stress in a healthy, productive way and connects them with people who have also been affected by pornography. The resource list at the back of the book offers many ideas for those interested in getting involved.

Most of the parents I meet want to protect their children from sexually explicit material but are simply unsure of how to do it. As parents apply even a few of the above-mentioned suggestions, they can make a tremendous difference in their children's life. Parents need not feel alone in this effort; there are a growing number of organizations and resources available to assist them. Having volunteered and consulted with many prodecency organizations and coalitions, I know from firsthand experience that these groups are very willing and uniquely qualified to help you in your worthy efforts.

Talking Points for Each Chapter

Chapter 1: What Is Pornography?
- How do you define pornography?
- What types of media have exposed you or someone you know to pornography?
- How do you feel about people making money from manipulating people's sexual feelings?

Chapter 2: What's the Big Deal about Pornography Today?
- Why do you believe pornography has dramatically increased in volume?
- How have you personally witnessed pornography's growing influence in our culture?
- How is Internet pornography different from other kinds of pornography?
- Why do these differences make Internet pornography a big deal?

Chapter 3: How Does Pornography Affect People?
- In your opinion, which effects of pornography are the most serious? Why?

- Were there any effects you had never heard of before? Which ones surprised you?
- Can you think of any real-life examples of people who experienced some of these effects?
- Did reading the list of researched effects shift your view of pornography at all?
- Are there any effects you would add to the list?

Chapter 4: Can Pornography Teach Me Things about Sexuality That I Need to Know in the Future?

- When did you first talk about sex with a parent or family member?
- What was that conversation like for you?
- How are questions about sexuality handled in your family? Does one parent usually answer all the questions, or is there a book your family refers to?
- What are some questions about sexuality that you are curious about and haven't had answered yet?
- Other than parents, where can you turn for accurate information about sexuality?

Chapter 5: What Should I Do If I Am Accidentally Exposed to Pornography?

- When have you been exposed to pornography?
- How did you handle that exposure at the time?

- What would you do differently today?
- Is there anything that you as a parent/teen team could do to help one another out when accidental exposures arise?

Chapter 6: What Should I Do If I Can't Stop Looking at Pornography?

- Which suggestions in this chapter do you think could help you the most?
- Do you know of someone who has been successful in overcoming a problem with pornography? If yes, what did he or she do to overcome it?
- If you don't have a problem with pornography, how can the suggestions in this chapter help you to live a healthier life?

Chapter 7: What Should I Do If I Know Someone Who Can't Stop Looking at Pornography?

- Are you concerned about someone who may have a problem with pornography use?
- How have you handled those concerns?
- What worked and what didn't?
- Which ideas in this chapter seem to be the most useful and doable for you?
- Based upon your own experience, what advice would you give young adults and parents who suspect or know someone is involved with pornography?

9
Conclusion

"We ought to be persuaded that the . . . smiles of heaven can never be expected on a nation that disregards the eternal rules of order and right which heaven itself has ordained."

—George Washington

Every generation has a battle or issue that defines the character, will, and spirit of that generation. Sometimes it is a war, a revolution, a natural disaster, or a moral dilemma that offers the opportunity for a generation to speak up, rise up, or make change, but again and again history teaches us that each generation is known for "something." I believe the plague of pornography is one of the defining issues that will test and define the Internet generation. We have important choices ahead of us. Will we preserve the freedoms we cherish while at the same time preserving our freedom to protect ourselves and our families from lies, distortions, and addictive material? I believe we are up for the challenge, even though it may seem that the odds are not in our favor.

My hope is that the Internet generation will come to recognize the lies they are being sold through pornography and come to see the devastating impact this material is having on many areas of life and society. I also hope that the parents of the Internet generation will teach and model healthy sexuality in such a way that our youth will have greater immunity to the sexual lies that bombard them in ever-increasing volume and at ever-increasing speed. Each young person deserves the best chance possible of achieving healthy, enduring, and joyful relationships in their future, but in the world we currently live in, each one will need significant support and guidance along the path to these types of relationships.

I have a great deal of faith in our youth, our parents, and our families to come up with creative and practical solutions to the problems we face. I, along with my own family, will lend support in any way we can to this cause. The plague of pornography is a *very big deal* that we cannot afford to ignore.

Resources

Helpful Organizations

1. For the treatment of pornography problems and/or sexually compulsive and addictive behavior

The *Life*STAR Network (teen and adult programs available)
   www.lifestarnetwork.org

Society for the Advancement of Sexual Health (SASH)
   www.sash.net

Faithful and True Ministries, Inc.
   www.faithfulandtrueministries.com

Sex Addicts Anonymous (SAA)
   www.sexaa.org

Sexaholics Anonymous (SA)
   www.sa.org

2. For information and training regarding Internet safety

Enough Is Enough
   www.enough.org

NetSmartz
www.netsmartzkids.org

Safe Kids
www.safekids.com

i-Safe
www.isafe.org

Internet Filter Review
www.internet-filter-review.com

Pause Parent Play
www.pauseparentplay.org

Communities for Decency
www.communitiesfordecency.org

3. For information on how to report Internet crime, harassment, child pornography, and/or sexual solicitation

National Center for Missing and Exploited Children
www.missingkids.com

The National Coalition for the Protection of Children and Families
www.nationalcoalition.org
Help line 1–800–583–2964 or (513) 521–6227

Cyber Angels
www.cyberangels.org

National Law Center for Children and Families
www.nationallawcenter.org

4. For information on how to combat pornography in your community or state

CP80
www.cp80.org

Communities for Decency
www.communitiesfordecency.org

Traffic Control: The People's War on Internet Pornography [DVD]
www.trafficcontrolthemovie.com

Utah Coalition Against Pornography
www.utahcoalition.org

5. For information on healthy sexuality

Kids Health
www.kidshealth.org (includes sections for kids, teens, and parents)

American Academy of Pediatrics
www.aap.org

Helpful Books

1. For information about overcoming pornography problems

Cybersex Unhooked: A Workbook for Breaking Free of Compulsive Online Sexual Behavior, by David L. Delmonico, Elizabeth Griffin, and Joseph Moriarity (Wickenburg, AZ: Gentle Path Press, 2001).

Healing the Wounds of Sexual Addiction, by Mark Laaser (Grand Rapids, MI: Zondervan, 2004).

Home Invasion: Protecting Your Family in a Culture That's Gone Stark Raving Mad, by Rebecca Hagelin (Nashville: Thomas Nelson, 2005).

In the Shadows of the Net: Breaking Free of Compulsive Online Sexual Behavior, by Patrick Carnes, David L. Delmonico, and Elizabeth Griffin (Center City, MN: Hazelden, 2004).

MySpace Unraveled: A Parent's Guide to Teen Social Networking, by Larry Magid and Anne Collier (Berkeley: Peachpit Press, 2006).

Protecting Your Child in an X-Rated World: What You Need to Know to Make a Difference, by Frank York and Jan LaRue (Wheaton, Illinois: Tyndale House Publishers, 2002).

2. For information about pornography and its impact

The Drug of the New Millennium: The Science of How Internet Pornography Radically Alters the Human Brain and Body, by Mark B. Kastleman (Orem, Utah: Granite Publishing, 2001).

The Impact of Internet Pornography on Marriage and the Family: A Review of the Research, by Jill C. Manning. Can be retrieved at http://heritage.org/Research/Family/upload/85273_1.pdf.

Pornified: How Pornography Is Transforming Our Lives, Our Relationships, and Our Families, by Pamela Paul (New York: Times Books and Henry Holt and Company, 2005).

3. For information about healthy sexuality

Growing Up: Gospel Answers about Maturation and Sex, by Brad Wilcox (Salt Lake City: Deseret Book, 2000).

How to Talk to Your Child about Sex, by Linda J. Eyre and Richard M. Eyre (New York: St. Martin's Press, 1998).

How to Talk with Teens about Love, Relationships and S-E-X: A Guide for Parents, by Amy G. Miron and Charles D. Miron (Minneapolis: Free Spirit Publishing, 2002).

How and When to Tell Your Kids about Sex: A Lifelong Approach to Shaping Your Child's Sexual Character, by Brenna Jones and Stan Jones (Colorado Springs: Navpress Publishing Group, 2007).

It's Perfectly Normal: Changing Bodies, Growing Up, Sex and Sexual Health, by Robie H. Harris (Cambridge, MA: Candlewick, 2004).

Questions Kids Ask about Sex: Honest Answers for Every Age, edited by Melissa R. Cox and the Medical Institute for Sexual Health (Grand Rapids, MI: Revell, 2007).

Sex and Sensibility: The Thinking Parent's Guide to Talking Sense about Sex, by Deborah M. Roffman (Cambridge, MA: Perseus Publishing, 2001).

Ten Talks Parents Must Have with Their Children about Sex and Character, by Pepper Schwartz and Dominic Cappello (New York: Hyperion, 2000).

The "What's Happening to My Body?" Book for Boys: A Growing-up Guide for Parents and Sons, Lynda Madaras and Area Madaras (New York: Newmarket, 2007).

The "What's Happening to My Body?" Book for Girls: A Growing-up Guide for Parents and Daughters, by Lynda Madaras and Area Madaras (New York: Newmarket, 2007).

Notes

1. Excerpt from Shelley Lubben's upcoming book, *The Truth behind the Fantasy of Porn.*

2. J. C. Manning, "The Impact of Internet Pornography on Marriage and the Family," 131–65.

3. E. Häggström-Nordin, U. Hanson, and T. Tydén, "Associations between Pornography Consumption and Sexual Practices among Adolescents in Sweden," 102–7.

4. C. Von Feilitzen and U. Carlsson, *Children in the New Media Landscape.*

5. K. J. Mitchell, D. Finkelhor, and J. Wolak, "Victimization of Youths on the Internet," 1–39.

6. M. Flood and C. Hamilton, "Youth and Pornography in Australia: Evidence on the Extent of Exposure and Likely Effects," The Australia Institute, Discussion Paper Number 52, ISSN 1322–5421.

7. Retrieved from the CP80 Foundation at www.cp80.org, April 6, 2007.

8. Ibid.

9. Retrieved from www.internet-filter-review.com, August 27, 2007.

10. Ibid.

11. Internet Filter Review, www.internet-filter-review.com, April 18, 2007.

12. P. Paul, "The Porn Factor," 99–100.

13. J. M. LaRue, Chief Counsel for Concerned Women for America, *Obscenity and the First Amendment.*

14. A. Cooper, "Online Sexual Activity in the New Millennium," i–vii.

15. Retrieved from www.internet-filter-review.com, August 25, 2007.

16. Ibid.

17. J. C. Manning, "The Impact of Internet Pornography on Marriage and the Family," 131–65.

18. J. Dedmon, "Is the Internet Bad for Your Marriage?"

19. Retrieved from CP80 Foundation, www.cp80.org, business effects page, April 25, 2007.

20. W. Koch, "Parolees on MySpace May Land in Jail," 1.

21. R. Kaslow and J. Robinson, "Long-term Satisfying Marriages," 69–78; J. Wallerstein and S. Blakeslee, *The Good Marriage*; F. Klagsburn, "Marriages That Last"; R. Levenson, L. Carstenson, and J. M. Gottman, "Long-term Marriage," 310–13; I. Wolcott, "Strong Families and Satisfying Marriages," 21–30.

22. See J. C. Manning, "The Impact of Internet Pornography on Marriage and the Family," 131–65 for the sources.

23. National Campaign to Prevent Teen Pregnancy, www .teenpregnancy.org.

24. T. B. Heaton, "Factors Contributing to Increasing Marital Stability in the United States," 392–409.

25. The B.L.A.H.S.T. acronym is commonly used in the *Life*STAR Network programs and literature.

26. A. Cooper, "Sexuality and the Internet," 181–87.

27. J. C. Manning, "The Impact of Internet Pornography on Marriage and the Family," 131–65.

28. K. J. Mitchell, D. Finkelhor, and J. Wolak, "Victimization of Youths on the Internet," 1–39.

29. Henry J. Kaiser Family Foundation Report.

30. Ibid.

31. Ibid.

32. K. J. Mitchell, D. Finkelhor, and J. Wolak, "Victimization of Youths on the Internet," 1–39.

33. J. D. Brown, "Mass Media Influences on Sexuality," 42–45.

34. L. C. Trostle, "Overrating Pornography As a Source of Sex Information for University Students," 143–50.

35. C. L. Somers and A. T. Surmann, "Adolescent's Preferences for Source of Sex Education," 47–59.

Bibliography

Buzzell, T. 2005. "The Effects of Sophistication, Access and Monitoring on Use of Pornography in Three Technological Contexts." *Deviant Behavior* 26:112.

Cooper, A. 1998. "Sexuality and the Internet: Surfing into the New Millennium." *CyberPsychology and Behavior* 1 (2): 181–87.

———. 2004. "Online Sexual Activity in the New Millennium." *Contemporary Sexuality* 38 (3): i–vii.

Dedmon, J. November 2002. "Is the Internet Bad for Your Marriage? Online Affairs, Pornographic Sites Playing Greater Role in Divorces." The Dilenschneider Group, press release.

Flood, M., and C. Hamilton. 2003. "Youth and Pornography in Australia: Evidence on the Extent of Exposure and Likely Effects." The Australia Institute, Discussion Paper Number 52, ISSN 1322–5421.

Häggström-Nordin, E., U. Hanson, and T. Tydén. 2005. "Associations between Pornography Consumption and Sexual Practices among Adolescents in Sweden." *International Journal of STD and AIDS* 16 (2): 102–7.

Heaton, T. B. 2002. "Factors Contributing to Increasing Marital Stability in the United States." *Journal of Family Issues* 23:392–409.

Henry J. Kaiser Family Foundation Report. 2002. Retrieved May 24,

2005, from http://www.kff.org/entmedia/loader.cfm?url=/com
monspot/security/getfile.cfm&PageID=14095.

Hinckley, G. B. 2000. *Standing for Something: 10 Neglected Virtues That
Will Heal Our Hearts and Homes.* New York: Three Rivers Press.

Kaslow, R., and J. Robinson. 1996. "Long-term Satisfying Marriages:
Perceptions of Contributing Factors." *American Journal of Family
Therapy* 24 (2): 69–78.

Klagsburn, F. 1995. "Marriages That Last." In J. Rank and E. Kain, eds.
Diversity and Change in Families: Patterns, Prospects, and Policies.
Englewood Cliffs, N.J.: Prentice Hall.

Koch, W. June 5, 2007. "Parolees on MySpace May Land in Jail." *USA
Today*, 1.

LaRue, J. M. 2005. *Obscenity and the First Amendment.* Summit on
Pornography, Washington, D.C., Rayburn House Office
Building, Room 2322, May 19, 2005.

Levenson, R., L. Carstenson, and J. M. Gottman. 1993. "Long-term
Marriage: Age, Gender, and Satisfaction." *Psychology and Aging* 8
(2): 310–13.

Lubben, Shelley. *The Truth behind the Fantasy of Porn*, retrieved from
http://www.shelleylubben.com, August 25, 2007.

Manning, J. C. 2006. "The Impact of Internet Pornography on
Marriage and the Family: A Review of the Research." *Sexual
Addiction and Compulsivity: The Journal of Treatment and Prevention*
13:131–65.

McGinnis, E. "The Horrifying Reality of Sex Trafficking." Retrieved
June 13, 2007, from http://www.beverlylahayeinstitute.org.

Mindel, A. 2005. Wordtracker report. Personal communication, June
21, 2005.

Mitchell, K. J., D. Finkelhor, and J. Wolak. 2003. "Victimization of
Youths on the Internet." In *The Victimization of Children: Emerging
Issues* (2003). J. L. Mullings, J. W. Marquart, D. J. Hartley, eds.
Binghamton, NY: Haworth Maltreatment and Trauma Press.

Paul, P. 2004. "The Porn Factor." *Time* 163 (3): 99–100.

————. 2005. *Pornified: How Pornography Is Transforming Our Lives, Our Relationships, and Our Families.* New York: Times Books and Henry Holt and Company.

Shapiro, B. 2005. *Porn Generation: How Social Liberalism Is Corrupting Our Future.* Washington, D.C.: Regnery.

Somers, C. L., and A. T. Surmann. 2004. "Adolescents' Preferences for Source of Sex Education." *Child Study Journal* 34 (1): 47–59.

Spink, A., and H. C. Ozmutlu. 2002. "Characteristics of Question Format Web Queries: An Exploratory Study." *Information Processing and Management* 38:453–71.

Stanley, J. 2001. "Child Abuse and the Internet." *National Child Protection Clearinghouse* 15:1–18.

Third Way Culture Project. 2005. "The Porn Standard: Children and Pornography on the Internet." Retrieved August 3, 2005, from www.third-way.com.

Trostle, L. C. 2003. "Overrating Pornography As a Source of Sex Information for University Students: Additional Consistent Findings." *Psychological Reports* 92:143–50.

Von Feilitzen, C., and U. Carlsson. 2000. *Children in the New Media Landscape: Games, Pornography, Perceptions.* Goteburg, Sweden: UNESCO/Nordicom.

Wallerstein, J., and S. Blakeslee. 1995. *The Good Marriage.* New York: Warner Books.

Watson, W. L. 2003. *Rock Solid Relationships: Strengthening Personal Relationships with Wisdom from the Scriptures.* Salt Lake City: Deseret Book.

"Web Traffic." 2004. *World Watch* 17 (6): 40.

Webster's Dictionary. 1984. Ninth New Collegiate Edition. Springfield, IL: Merriam-Webster, Inc.

Wolcott, I. 1999. "Strong Families and Satisfying Marriages." *Family Matters* 53:21–30.

York, F., and J. LaRue. 2002. *Protecting Your Child in an X-Rated World.* Wheaton, Illinois: Tyndale House Publishers.

Index

About the Author

Jill C. Manning, Ph.D., is a licensed marriage and family therapist who specializes in research and clinical work related to pornography and problematic sexual behavior. Dr. Manning has been featured in television programs, documentaries, and radio talk shows and has authored numerous book chapters and academic journal articles on the subject of pornography. In 2005, Dr. Manning was selected to be a visiting social science fellow at The Heritage Foundation in Washington, D.C., and, as a result of her research there, testified before a Senate subcommittee on the harms of pornography. A native of Calgary, Alberta, Canada, she currently resides in Denver, Colorado, with her husband.